T0305931

LEADER WORK

Leader Work offers an accessible and engaging introduction to the power of reflection to support leaders in their development and professional practice. The book does not present a tick-box toolkit to being a better leader, instead it provides the prompts and deeper reflexive space for leaders to consider their own self-development.

Written by a leading management researcher and consultant, the book draws on reflexive practice, but goes beyond this method to guide the reader on how to consider both inward and outward work, and provides useful suggestions for application. The inward work involves developing our knowledge of ourselves, our capabilities and our limitations through self-examination and connecting with others, and so building up our capacity for judgment, and gaining confidence in using intuition and imagination thoughtfully in situations of complexity and uncertainty. The outward work involves learning to express a leader identity that is both true to ourselves and recognized by relevant groups and the organizations in which we work, so that we are trusted to help navigate and narrate a path through uncertainty.

This book has been written for leaders and would-be leaders looking to develop and shape their practice, as well as scholars studying and teaching leadership classes.

Paul Hibbert is Professor of Management at the University of Warwick, UK, where he leads the Organization and Work Group. His career also encompasses leadership roles at the University of St Andrews and professional associations, and working with a wide range of organizations in consultancy, training and professional development roles.

"This rigorous, diligent and inspired writing on leadership work is a page turner – not least because it creates an empathy with the reader through the challenges of leadership, right from the beginning of the book. This holistic approach to doing leadership, alongside the continuous work of trying to do it the best we can, makes explicit all of our very human, institutional and resource constraints in tow. Hibbert brings the holistic self (mind, body, emotion, practice) of what it means to do leadership work to life. Reflecting on his personal experiences he reveals theory in action. At the same time, the open and reflexive nature of his writing manages to balance straightforward 'here's something to think about that might help you' advice with a recognition of the complex and dynamic nature of what it means to lead. In Hibbert's presentation, we all experience moments of leadership – opportunities where we can step forward and act in particularly uncertain landscapes. As such, we are always becoming – as is our organisational culture and identity through our reflexive actions. This book is a 'must-read' for anyone faced with the challenges and opportunities of leadership, as well as for those interested in developing theoretical approaches to the whole and multiple selves made up through leadership action."

Professor Katy Mason, *Professor of Markets, Marketing and Management, Lancaster University, and President of the British Academy of Management*

"In a market that is flooded with 'how-to' guides, *Leader Work* stands out by its thoroughly researched and evidence-based road map for leaders to develop leadership practice. Paul Hibbert masterfully charts how combining internal and external forms of work allows leaders to take responsibility for leadership, and to be recognized as the right person to lead when it matters most. The book makes a compelling call for leaders who show strength in different, more thoughtful, self-aware and compassionate ways – and provides important insights to help those who find themselves leading to know how to do that. *Leader Work* should be required reading for any leader facing the challenges of leading in the complex and uncertain environments which have increasingly become the norm."

Professor David Collings, *Chair of Sustainable Business, Trinity Business School, Trinity College Dublin*

"*Leader Work* is a must-read, inspiring guide to developing reflexive practice for leaders. If you want to develop your leadership practice through self-awareness and reflexivity, Paul Hibbert provides accessible explanations and practical provocations for leaders to work on themselves – you can focus on individual chapters as your learning unfolds. Focusing on reflexive practice through embodiment, emotions, thought, relationships, and identity work, this is an excellent resource for leaders and a welcome addition for those facilitating leadership development — it brings new energy and innovative thinking to reflexive practice and leadership."

Professor Sharon Mavin, *Professor of Leadership and Organization Studies, Newcastle University Business School*

"Paul Hibbert's book on leader work reminds us that leadership cannot be attributed to certain traits or characteristics; rather, Hibbert makes a strong case that leader success can be attributed to inward and outward forms of leader work. Hibbert describes how a set of reflexive practice tools on multiple levels — embodied, emotional, thoughtful, and relational — can provide insight and confidence that allows one to lead in a way that feels authentic. *Leader Work: Using Insight, Intuition and Imagination to Develop Leadership Practice* is a book for thoughtful leaders who wish to improve their impact, aspiring leaders who are honing their leadership skills and individuals who wonder if they are cut out for leadership (the answer is yes!). Readers who are willing to engage in the creative, and sometimes uncomfortable, exercises provided by the author will likely have their views of leadership challenged while simultaneously becoming better leaders. I definitely recommend this book for business executives and aspiring leaders of all occupations."

Professor Sherry M.B. Thatcher, *Regal Entertainment Distinguished Professor, Haslam College of Business, University of Tennessee, Knoxville, and Editor in Chief of Academy of Management Review*

LEADER WORK

Using Insight, Intuition and Imagination to Develop Leadership Practice

Paul Hibbert

Routledge
Taylor & Francis Group

LONDON AND NEW YORK

Designed cover image: © Getty Images / wildpixel

First published 2024
by Routledge
4 Park Square, Milton Park, Abingdon, Oxon OX14 4RN

and by Routledge
605 Third Avenue, New York, NY 10158

Routledge is an imprint of the Taylor & Francis Group, an informa business

© 2024 Paul Hibbert

The right of Paul Hibbert to be identified as author of this work has been asserted in accordance with sections 77 and 78 of the Copyright, Designs and Patents Act 1988.

British Library Cataloguing-in-Publication Data
A catalogue record for this book is available from the British Library

Library of Congress Cataloging-in-Publication Data
Names: Hibbert, Paul, author.
Title: Leader work : using insight, intuition and imagination to develop leadership practice / Paul Hibbert.
Description: Abingdon, Oxon ; New York, NY : Routledge, 2024. | Includes bibliographical references and index.
Identifiers: LCCN 2023047873 (print) | LCCN 6502023047874 (ebook) | ISBN 9781032721491 (hardback) | ISBN 9781032693064 (paperback) | ISBN 9781032721507 (ebook)
Subjects: LCSH: Leadership.
Classification: LCC HD57.7 .H537 2024 (print) | LCC HD57.7 (ebook) | DDC 658.4/092—dc23/eng/20231026
LC record available at https://lccn.loc.gov/2023047873
LC ebook record available at https://lccn.loc.gov/2023047874

ISBN: 978-1-032-72149-1 (hbk)
ISBN: 978-1-032-69306-4 (pbk)
ISBN: 978-1-032-72150-7 (ebk)

DOI: 10.4324/9781032721507

Typeset in Joanna
by codeMantra

CONTENTS

ACKNOWLEDGMENTS

We achieve nothing by ourselves. This book is no exception, and owes its existence to two groups of people: those who have inspired and partnered me in my research on reflexive practice and those who have shown me what leader work really looks like.

Enormous thanks to my friends and partners in reflexive research projects: Nic Beech, Lisa Callagher, Christine Coupland, Ann Cunliffe, Ziad Elsahn, Ben Hardy, Stefan Korber, Robert Macintosh, Sharon Mavin and Frank Siedlok. I have learned so much from working with you all – not least about myself – and benefitted from your kindness in innumerable ways.

Grateful thanks too to those who have shown me wonderful examples of leader work in their careers, which includes my research partners and friends Nic Beech and Sharon Mavin, and my inspirational friends Peter McNamara at the University of Maynooth and Lorna Milne at the University of St Andrews. I started to write about all the ways I have learned from you in these brief acknowledgments, but I realized it would take another full chapter!

My heartfelt thanks to all of you, and to all the people I had the privilege of offering leadership to at the University of St Andrews, in the Academy of Management and during my career in industry.

While this book has benefitted from the insights of so many good people, any errors and omissions are all my own.

1

INTRODUCTION

LEADER WORK POSSIBILITIES

Leader work

If you are involved in leadership roles, you know that your work involves dealing with uncertainty. In the face of the unknown, it can be a struggle to have confidence about our future direction, and how to guide others along the way. So what can we do? We can get a better handle on our limits, develop an ability to cope with incomplete understanding and grow to be ready to help others find a way to go forward. This is the essence of how leadership is described by Ganz (2010): it is focused on taking responsibility for helping a group to work towards a shared objective, when the way ahead is uncertain. This means that leader work can be done by anyone who can take responsibility in the moment, when there is a particular reason. To help explain what this looks like, here is an example from my own experience.

DOI: 10.4324/9781032721507-1

A PERSONAL STORY: A MOMENT OF LEADER WORK

I was working for the vice-principal in charge of education, at a time when students had ranked us in the top five full-range universities for a number of years. But one year, we dropped from 1st to 25th in the national survey. This was a survival issue, since our reputation for excellent teaching was pivotal to attracting students. Early one morning, soon after the results were published, I saw my boss looking really worried. "What's up?" I asked.

"I have to meet the Principal at 12, with a plan to turn around the student rankings. I don't have one," she replied.

We both knew that the meeting would be ... uncomfortable, to say the least. I thought I could do something to help. What was needed was a plan that got us started: it didn't have to be perfect, but it did have to lead to a process that could work. I knew I was good at planning and intuitively thought that a process based on guided learning might help to address the difficult results in the student survey. I cancelled my meetings for the morning and set to work. Two hours later I had an outline plan for a learning process across the university, with timelines for implementation to deliver change ahead of the next national survey. My boss made some adjustments to the plan and presented it at the midday meeting, which went well.

The process worked well, too. The next year we were back in the number 1 spot in the rankings for full-range universities.

In the example, an opportunity for leader work arose when I realized that I had some insights (along with some intuition, of which more later) that could help to plot a course through a worrying time of uncertainty. It is important to note that I was not asked to take action, but instead recognized the opportunity and took it: this was just a focal moment for me in a process that relied on a lot of leader work and management action from others. Most observers would say that it was my boss that made the plan work in practice, and I would agree. This reinforces the point that leader work is not tied to a formal role, and while it is required to handle times of uncertainty, it is *not necessarily* required at other times. I wasn't stepping in to provide suggested plans every day! If conditions are relatively stable and the choice about how to act is clear, then that requires management action rather than leadership (Wolfram Cox & Hassard, 2018). The trouble is, of course, that uncertainty seems to be becoming the normal condition of the world, and everyone in it.

When leadership is needed, under conditions of uncertainty and the difficult complexity it usually entails, it is concerned with how one person influences the actions, behaviors or choices of others in ways that do not (necessarily) involve the overt use of power or management control (Hibbert, 2015). People can influence others in non-directive ways when there is some shared goal that they all buy into, although leadership is usually involved in creating the goal, too. Approaches vary; some leaders may seek to influence through being ethically sound and authentic (Algera & Lips-Wiersma, 2012), some through espousing service to a community rather than dominating it (Mittal & Dorfman, 2012) and some through taking advantage of the persistent and widespread public fascination with charisma (Hibbert & Cunliffe, 2015). The charismatic (or heroic: Fourie, 2023) view sees leadership as a permanent, always-on attribute of special individuals. However, there are good reasons for challenging the charismatic or heroic view: leadership is not always needed at a particular moment in time (Ganz, 2010), the right individual to provide it within a group may change depending on the context (Hibbert, 2015) and organizations, groups and communities can all be ambivalent about whether they want to be led or not (Sydow, Lerch, Huxham & Hibbert, 2011). Thus, it makes no sense to think of leadership as a fixed and one-dimensional character attribute. Instead, it is a task or form of work. Such work is possible when we have sufficient and justified confidence to act, in a certain context, and we can combine that confidence with the ability to be recognized as the right person to offer guidance at that time. These conditions support *leader work*, which I define more fully in the following way.

•

> Leader work combines inward and outward forms of work. The inward work involves developing our knowledge of ourselves, our capabilities and our limitations through self-examination and connecting with others; building up our capacity for judgment; and gaining confidence in using intuition and imagination thoughtfully in situations of complexity and uncertainty. The outward work involves learning to express a leader identity that is both true to ourselves and recognized by relevant groups and organizations, so that we are trusted to help them navigate and narrate a path through uncertainty.

The definition of leader work is explored and explained across the course of the book, and I will return to it in the Conclusion. For now, the key point is that undertaking the two forms of leader work – inward and outward – allows you to take responsibility for leadership, and to be recognized as the right person to do so, when it matters. Leader work supports the activities that influence others, especially using your knowledge, intuition and imagination to craft a way forward when the right path is uncertain, and acting as a personal example for others. It may also involve combining these approaches to bring others into the leadership space (Hibbert, 2015). The ability to use effective communication, exemplary action and empowered involvement are reliant on interpreting our experience in order to understand what is going on in a particular situation, so that we can develop ideas about what approaches and tools might help us to lead in that context (Cunliffe & Hibbert, 2016; Hibbert, Beech & Siedlok, 2017). Interpretation is going on from "the other side" of leadership too, and as an intrinsic part of this interpretation, people judge the messenger as well as the message. We all do this. Think about the popular television program *The Voice*. The whole premise of the show is that talent-spotting judges can only focus on the quality of a singer's voice – without being influenced by their looks – because they are prevented from seeing the singers before picking them. But if you watch the show, you will notice how some of the judges are delighted when they find they have picked someone who turns out to be young and conventionally attractive. In addition, even before pressing the button to show they want to pick the unseen singer, some judges may scan the reactions of the audience (who *can* see the singer), to see what *they* think of them!

On a more general and subtle level we all find ourselves influenced by the person, and not just the things that they do, when they are trying to provide leadership. We don't stop to think about this: we are always already interpreting and judging (Hibbert et al., 2017). Otherwise, why would people bother to dress up for job interviews, take part in legal proceedings or seek a political appointment? Similarly, people will also make judgments based on other aspects of ourselves that have no relationship to our ability to do a job, tell the truth or be worthy of election – like gender, ethnicity or sexuality, for example – and those interpretations and biases can get in the way of some of us taking on the roles that we wish, or prevent us from working in the ways that might be most effective for us (Callagher, Elsahn, Hibbert, Korber & Siedlok, 2021).

In short, when we act as leaders, we are influencing people through our identity – and the identity work we do to hold that self-presentation together (Beech, 2017) – as well as our actions. This is true whether we choose to influence people that way or not. This is perhaps why people are still fascinated and captivated by the idea of a strong charismatic leader (Hibbert & Cunliffe, 2015), who is usually male and often from a narrow ethnic range. Unfortunately, charismatic leaders are also, often, abominable. They have set the world aflame, more than once. And they continue to burn us through corruption, war and willful ignorance of an increasingly desperate climate crisis.

We need to ask for leadership that shows strength in different, more thoughtful, self-aware and compassionate ways, and help those who find themselves leading to know how to do that. It is not easy to be recognized and act persuasively when the moment for leadership comes. Shaping ourselves to be able to do this involves a learning challenge. The necessary learning includes a long-term process of formation (Hibbert et al., 2017) and ongoing reflexive practice (Hibbert, 2021a; Hibbert, Coupland & MacIntosh, 2010). Reflexive practice is concerned with paying attention to ourselves, our situations and how we are changing, in order to develop a better self-understanding and be more in control of the ways in which we learn, adapt and change in the future.

Reflexive practice is a key theme in this book, and is critical to understanding how we can prepare to engage in leader work and know what that involves. However, reflexive practice needs to be combined with other practices and processes. Thus, overall, there are four key things that are explained in this book. An overview of each is provided in the remainder of this introduction. First, I will explain the process of formation, and the ways in which that process involves unexpected forms of learning that can support reflexive practice (Hibbert, 2021a). Second, I explore how we are *always* changing (even if we wish we were not), and what that can mean for us when we capture it through different levels of reflexive practice. This also leads to insights about how we can support and develop leader work directly through these levels of reflexive practice. Third, I consider how we can use the self-knowledge gained through integrating insights from all of the levels of reflexive practice. Above all, this self-knowledge helps us to act and present our identity coherently, in ways that help us to be recognized as leaders when it is necessary. Fourth, I consider a pivotal integrative challenge for leader work: the need to be able to craft persuasive stories, which provide a trust-supporting picture of who we are and a clear direction for the future, while also keeping the possibilities for learning and change open. This balance of story-telling and inquiry is essential: our stories, and those of the organizations where we conduct our leader work, will continue to develop and we need to be able to capture new developments and weave them into the narrative. After these four main points have been addressed, this opening chapter concludes with a brief discussion about how to apply the ideas offered in this book.

Learning and formation for leader work

One of the most important things to know about leadership and leader work is that they involve continued learning. That includes the lessons gathered from inevitable mistakes. This is because, as I emphasized earlier, leadership is only really needed when the context and situation convey uncertainty about the way forward (Ganz, 2010). If there is a clear and straightforward answer to the question "what should we do?" then you have a management task ahead of you (Wolfram Cox & Hassard, 2018), instead of a need for leader work. Importantly, this means that the kind of learning that is needed for leader work is not technical and precise. Instead, learning to deal with uncertainty and unpredictability calls for broad, generalist learning and a slow and continuing process of formation that leads to a capacity for judgment (Epstein, 2020; Hibbert et al., 2017).

How does a broad, generalist process of formation help? It does not eliminate uncertainty through loading us up with knowledge and technical skills to fill in all the possible gaps. Instead, formation helps us to be more comfortable with not knowing. This aligns with Allen's (2017) picture of reflexive practice and learning, which explains how it is possible to accept that not knowing is a persistent human condition and that some level of anxiety and uncertainty is normal. But, by acknowledging the normality of that condition, we can focus on what might be possible and avoid ramping up the anxiety by aiming for a level of certainty we can never reach. Over time, we develop our ability to cope and act in the face of unpredictable conditions, not by developing perfect knowledge but by learning to recognize what feels right.

The process of formation, which helps us to recognize what feels right, embraces a wide range of possibilities, but there are some essential features within it. Hibbert et al. (2017) argue that the process of formation has three key aspects. The first aspect of the process is stretched out over time and can be described as the *long-term experience of interpretation*. Through a deliberate engagement with a broad range of sources of meaning and insight over extended periods, and with content stretching far beyond technical or professional material, we learn to make sense of or become intuitively aware of complex patterns (Epstein, 2020; Gigerenzer, 2008). Developing this ability to deal with incomplete knowledge and complexity involves the growth of the whole person, and it may involve engagement with art, literature and other cultural sources alongside "normal" professional training. The value of a broad and non-utilitarian education means that what you engage in as a personal interest may be just as important as your vocational learning in the process of formation. Along these lines, a rationale is offered by Epstein (2020), who provides a persuasive account of how breadth in our patterns of self-development can lead to an ability to cope with uncertainty and "wicked" learning contexts: one of the keys to these abilities is the capacity for creativity, in generating new insights and solutions. Epstein (2020) describes how, surprisingly, the most creative and path-breaking scientists and scholars are not monomaniacs purely focused on their discipline. Instead, they are much more likely than the average scientist to have a range of interests in the arts, music and the performing arts, whether creating new works or participating in performances. And the higher the level of achievement, the more likely it is that scientists will have these other interests – with Nobel Prize winners being the most likely of all to have this breadth. In contrast, average scientists and members of the public are both less likely to have such broad interests.

There is obviously a breadth of creative capacity that comes from having interests beyond the focus of our careers, vocations or professions. It is also the case that the useful learning that you gain in this way is not likely to be intentional or purposive; instead, it comes from the interests and experiences we commit to for genuine enjoyment or meaning and not for their usefulness (which is unpredictable and emergent). Thus, gaining a breadth of experience clearly matters, and it supports creativity and insight: we learn to find meaning in ways that we would otherwise miss, and our everyday experience is enriched by these alternative ways of seeing.

While experience has long been recognized as a pivotal source for leadership development (Benjamin & O'Reilly, 2011; Casey & Goldman, 2010; Ligon, Hunter & Mumford, 2008), in general leadership development has been concerned with pivotal life experiences and/or emphasis on genuine encounters with the "real problems" that leaders encounter (Benjamin & O'Reilly, 2011; Ligon et al., 2008). However, as Hibbert et al. (2017) and Epstein (2020) establish, a much wider range of experiences – which need not be concerned with real situations or work problems – can be useful in building up the capacity to cope with uncertainty. This is because a breadth of experience supports the creativity and willingness to "fill in the gaps" in uncertain situations using intuition and imagination, rather than relying on our familiar knowledge and ways of going about things.

However, experience of interpretation across a broad range of interests is more useful to us in the long term, for our formation and self-development, if we also focus on *interpretation in the moment*. This second aspect of a process of formation requires us to be reflexive about the influences on our general self-development, as we encounter them. We may be captivated by ideas, images and thoughts in an aesthetic way (Gadamer, 1998) – they simply appeal to us in ways we cannot quite decode – as we encounter them in our everyday lives. To get behind this encounter with something captivating, we first need to *notice* that we have been captivated, or perhaps been "struck" by something unexpected or unsettling. Cunliffe (2002) explains that "being struck" involves a sense of some new insight that we cannot grasp directly in the moment. Being struck is not a prompt to search out some new source of knowledge to explain what is going on, but instead an invitation – at least at first – to look within, to focus on what is "going on" in our experience in the moment.

The invitation to look within is another aspect of finding a way to go on despite uncertainty – we find possibilities and questions that shape our actions going forward. As we live out those new possibilities, we may find that our somewhat intuitive sense of what feels right leads to clearer forms of knowledge, at least some of the time. Nevertheless, the most important first step is not to seek out concrete knowledge, once we notice that we have been "struck" or captivated. As Cunliffe (2002) points out, instead we need to be able to explore the experience from within in order to engage critically with all the ways that it has impacted on us. That engagement requires a lot of attention, in more forms than we might expect. It involves being appreciatively aware that we interpret with and through our *bodies, emotions* and *thoughts* (that have been shaped by our past) and to add to this, we gather critical insights through our *relationships* (Hibbert, 2021a).

The third part of the process of formation is, therefore, to learn in different ways through *relationships* in reflexive dialogue (Hibbert et al., 2017; Hibbert, Siedlok & Beech, 2016). Reflexive dialogue provides a route to exploring different ways of seeing and understanding the world and our concerns, through conversations with others. Having brought to bear our full personal capacity for awareness on all levels, we connect with others to complement and challenge our knowledge through seeing perspectives that are not clear from our own vantage point. Thus, as I will discuss extensively in later parts of the book, reflexive dialogue with others is a key practice in continued learning for leader work, whether as part of a process of formation or in the context of day-to-day uncertainties. As Corlett (2013, p467) explains, any situation in which we interact with others always includes possibilities for learning through dialogue, and we need to be ready to explore that potential when the moment of being struck is upon us. Others will always have insights that are not obvious to us. To put it another way, everyone who we engage in dialogue can show us something we could not otherwise see. As I shall explain later, the benefits of dialogue can even include new insights about ourselves. However, dialogue is just one form and level of reflexive practice. There is a need to consider, as I have already hinted, that *reflexive practice* on many levels – *embodied, emotional* and *thoughtful*, as well as the *relational* level of dialogue – is key to our formation and readiness for leader work. Indeed, reflexive practice at all levels is at the heart of this book, and I explain why that is the case in the following section.

Our changing selves: reflexive practice, self-understanding and leader work

The primary foundation, and the heart of learning for inward-focused leader work, is to understand how people who lead, manage or work in organizations (and that's pretty much most of us, at least for some of our lifetime) can be more aware of who we are, and how we change over time. It is important to note, at this point, that all of us are always changing, both consciously and unconsciously (Hibbert et al., 2010). Think how your younger self, just finishing high school, might react if they met the person you are today. Could you explain how you have come to be so different?[1] Our choices and experiences lead us to adapt in ways that we do not always expect, as do factors beyond our control.

Adaptation is thus a normal, and often automatic, part of life. However, we can develop our practice to be more deliberate about how we are changing (or resisting change – see Hibbert, Callagher, Siedlok, Windahl & Kim, 2019), and think about what that means for how we influence others. This complicated process of focusing on how we are affected and changed over time – while trying to make it less automatic or unconscious – is reflexive practice. Reflexive practice (Hibbert, 2021a) simply means, more or less, that we turn reflection inward to ask who we are, consider how we are changing and question our assumptions about why we do what we do now, rather than turning reflection outward to ask what to do next. Asking inward-focused questions leads us to realize that we experience change over time and interpret the world on multiple levels: specifically through our bodies, emotions, thoughts and relationships (Hibbert, 2021a). The different layers of experience that guide our adaptation are often overlapping, but we can understand them better by focusing on each one in turn. I do so in Chapters 2 to 5, each of which has a common structure: the nature of experience at each level is first discussed, followed by how that informs reflexive practice and then the implications and possibilities for leader work are set out. A summary of each of these chapters, and the different kinds of reflexive practice and leader work that they discuss, follows.

Embodied reflexive practice

As I explain in Chapter 2, the different kinds of signals we experience in our bodies have important effects on the way our emotions are experienced, may influence how our thoughts take shape and can affect how we interact with and understand other people. We are not used to considering our bodies as influences on our emotions, thoughts and relationships and, for most of us, some attention to these points is long overdue. To pay more attention we can develop and use our awareness, and become more at home in our bodies, through techniques like mindfulness (Williams & Penman, 2011) and centering (Walsh, 2021). These are simple techniques to name and discuss, but it is important to underline that these kinds of embodied reflexive practice need to be engaged in and not just understood, and different forms may be more or less appropriate for different people. However, if taken seriously they can have some positive benefits that are important for responding to leader work challenges.

One of the main benefits of embodied reflexive practice is that it helps us to show congruence, for example to use body language that is aligned with the confident and/or calm disposition that we are seeking to communicate through talk in our leader work (Palmer & Crawford, 2013). However, leader work also has to include making space for those for whom this kind of congruent presentation is not possible because of intense but transient personal problems (Kivenen, 2021) or more permanent differences (Higashida, 2013). If people are going through serious emotional crises or are not neurotypical, then congruence may be difficult for them: at such times the person with the difficulty is actually the observer – you, if you are not the person struggling – and making space for those who struggle with congruence is in your own interest as a leader too.

Emotional reflexive practice

I explain in Chapter 3 how emotions can affect us immediately, in a particular situation, or affect us later through (triggered) memories. In either case they alert us to some potential information about a situation (and perhaps ourselves) that it is worth gathering. As we collect that information, we need to take care to avoid the traps that firing up the wrong emotional response can lead us into. Sometimes we interpret our emotions as telling us to look away when they are trying to draw our attention to something, or confuse basic emotions (concerned with individual wellbeing, like fear) with moral emotions (concerned with what we feel is right or wrong in our life with others, like shame). Accordingly, I explain the process of engaging in emotional reflexive practice carefully in four steps: (1) attention to perceptions of our own and others' emotions; (2) reflection on the emotional history of the situation; (3) speculative exploration of the future emotional trajectory of the situation; and (4) exploring possible functional conflict issues (Giner-Sorolla, 2013, 2018), by considering whether the "wrong" function of moral emotions has been triggered if the story seems to make no sense or feels wrong. Spotting functional conflict is the trickiest aspect of emotional reflexive practice but it explains a lot of confusion and conflict in organizations to know that (1) people sometimes regulate their emotions when authentic expression would be more helpful (and vice versa) and (2) sometimes people make a snap emotional judgment rather than recognizing that unsettled emotions show us that something unusual is going on, something that needs thoughtful attention. However, all of the elements of emotional reflexive practice can feed into leader work.

Emotions are part of normal human interaction, but organizations often have climates which encourage or require us to keep our emotions suppressed or disguised: they are emotionally overregulated contexts. If we can get past that overregulation, emotional reflexive practice helps us to be aware of the value of the emotional messages that we send and receive, and may help us to legitimize and weave emotional (aspects of) stories into our leader identity (Hibbert, Beech, Callagher & Siedlok, 2022). This can also legitimize emotions in others' identity work, too, since it is not helpful to suppress – as organizations often do – the normal human emotional engagement in our self-expression (Muhr, De Cock, Twardowska & Volkmann, 2019; Soini and Eräranta 2023). Making more space for recognizing and working with emotions in organizations is therefore likely to support leader work, allowing us to engage people in a more human and humane story of who we are as a collective.

Thoughtful reflexive practice

In Chapter 4 I explain how thoughtful reflexive practice weaves together a critical perspective on the past that shaped us (Hibbert et al., 2010; Hibbert & Cunliffe, 2015) and an imaginative and intuitive engagement (Elbanna, 2015; Gigerenzer, 2008) with the future, which uses different ways of seeing and knowing. This leads to more alternative insights about how we interpret what is going on in a particular situation, which in turn gives us more options for future action and developing new understandings. These insights show how criticality, imagination and intuition have a role in thoughtful reflexive practice (Cunliffe, 2018) and related leader work. Strengthening these supports for leader work involves "resourcing" our imagination through engagement with art and literature (Hibbert et al., 2017), and building up our "negative capability" to cope with uncertainty and engaging in bricolage[2] through working with whatever information and insight is available.

It is important to note (as with embodied and emotional reflexive practice) that thoughtful, reflexive practice includes both "front-stage" short-term work in particular situations and "back-stage" longer-term work. The back-stage, longer-term work helps us to be ready for a range of situations in which we will encounter uncertainty about how to proceed. Overall, thoughtful reflexive practice helps us to be aware of the irreducible uncertainty in most contexts, and be able to take decisions and act anyway, through the right use of intuition, imagination and bricolage. Importantly, thoughtful reflexive practice can also lead to and support relational reflexive practice, when the uncertainties are too great for an independent decision (and perhaps when different conscious and unconscious motives are pulling us in different directions).

Relational reflexive practice

Relational reflexive practice, as I explain in Chapter 5, helps us to focus attention on how we interpret who we are, and how we struggle to know ourselves fully. Despite the insights we can draw from embodied, emotional and thoughtful reflexive practice, addressing the question of who we are requires a relational level of engagement. Through dialogue with others, through "conversations" with literature, and through interpreting our stories of ourselves, we can bring other perspectives to our situation through relational reflexive practice. These other perspectives help us to surface the non-conscious motivations and assumptions that may be at odds with the stories we tell about ourselves. Engaging with fiction emerges as a surprisingly helpful and almost universally accessible resource for this kind of reflexive practice, and there is good evidence for why this is so. Stories are more memorable than other forms of text (Mar, Li, Nguyen & Ta, 2021) and provide characters with whom we form imaginative close attachments (Rain & Mar, 2021). Because of this, stories help us to develop our ability to understand and have empathy with others (Mar, 2018), which in turn enables us to better engage, through trust-based dialogue, in relational reflexive practice with other people. In that situation of trust and dialogue, we are more open to learning new insights about ourselves. For all of us there is value in developing a coherent self-understanding and the ability to make trusting connections with others: this supports our everyday wellbeing as well as our leader work.

Identity work and leader work

As I explain in Chapters 2 to 5 and summarize above, the inward work of reflexive practice – at embodied, emotional, thoughtful and relational levels – directly supports some possibilities for leader work. However, reflexive practice across the four levels also supports a particularly important form of leader work: that is, leader identity work. Without reflexive practice, and in particular relational reflexive practice to explore our unacknowledged and unconscious aspects, we might not really know who we are. A lack of self-knowledge is also going to mean that we will be perceived differently than we expect. Thus, I discuss identity work in Chapter 6 after building up the necessary groundwork of reflexive practice in earlier chapters. Identity work concerns the moment-to-moment ways that we try to ensure that how we wish to see ourselves, in a particular place and at a particular time, is also how we are recognized by others (Beech, Gilmore, Hibbert & Ybema, 2016; Brown, 2015). Identity work is necessary to address the challenges and threats to our identity that we might experience, for example through discrimination (Callagher et al., 2021) or from more innocent motives and misunderstandings. Identity work can also have an ethical dimension beyond resisting discrimination and eliminating misunderstandings, through the presentation of ourselves or others as moral exemplars (Gill, 2023) who can influence others in positive ways.

Identity work supports influence in more than one way through the reception of our presentation of self in leader work. The ways in which our identity is received and understood can set the norms of self-expression for others, allowing rational concerns, basic emotions and moral emotions such as pride, shame, disgust or even "righteous anger" (Hibbert, 2023) to feature in their identity work. This is not to argue that we should see our rational selves and emotional selves almost as separate creatures: instead, it can be helpful to use the two lenses to help provide a better way of seeing a complete picture. Thus, Chapter 6 looks in more detail at the nature of identity work and how it is challenged, and considers in depth how basic and moral emotions are tied up in identity work. It also considers the ways in which identity work is involved in influencing others, often through the presentation of "prototypical" identities to support an established position. When we have an established position, then leader work to challenge and change identity norms in favor of diversity become possible.

Navigating and narrating the future

Our ability to tell a persuasive story of ourselves (implicitly or explicitly) is strongly connected to effective leader identity work. Chapter 7, the concluding chapter, builds on this connection to establish how individual self-narratives need to be worked out before embarking on projects to author an organizational narrative. An organizational narrative is a story that helps a collective to find a way forward in times of uncertainty (Ganz, 2010; Shoup & Hinrichs, 2021). To explain the effects and benefits of narrative, the chapter highlights the essential form of a story, explores how stories and narrative (the terms are often used interchangeably, though not by all scholars) have been related to individual and organizational purposes and considers how stories can be used to support leader work in a variety of organizations.

While organizational stories need to connect with the preferences of the organization members or social group on one level (Fourie, 2023; Ganz, Lee Cunningham, Ben Ezer & Segura, 2023), they also need to align with and accommodate the self-expression of the person undertaking leader work, as Chapter 7 explains. However, in the context of leader work, stories – whether they are about ourselves or an organization – are never written once and for all. Individuals, organizations and the world in which they participate all change over time. Leader work requires being aware of change and adapting to it, and helping the organization to change, too. As I outlined earlier, reflexive practice helps with change awareness on an individual level, while reflexive dialogue in particular can help to better inform adaptation and involve more people in the effort to understand and guide that process of change for ourselves and others (Hibbert, Sillince, Diefenbach & Cunliffe, 2014). Involvement in relational reflexive practice therefore has a double benefit. Thus, Chapter 7 emphasizes that the process of "writing" self- and organizational narratives needs to be balanced with "reading" new and emerging understandings and possibilities through reflexive dialogue, so that stories can continue to be refreshed to reflect new insights.

Application

It is my hope that others will develop and challenge the ideas in this book through adapting the ideas to their own ways of practicing in their own unique contexts, or perhaps develop alternative ideas through debate. However, I recognize that some readers using the book may be looking for starting points for their own practice. For that reason and for those readers, some possible actions that build on the insights of Chapters 2 to 6 are provided at the end of these chapters. If you are not interested in applying the ideas in each chapter at the time you can always skip these sections and return to them later, if and when you find it helpful to do so. Similarly, the longer-term integrative work of developing stories through leader work, which is described in Chapter 7, is balanced by a summary of some short-term leadership tactics (Fourie, 2023) and reflexive rules of thumb (Hibbert, 2021a) in the closing part of that chapter. Leader work has to include momentary changes of direction as well as plotting courses over the long term.

With plotting a course in mind, it is in the nature of a conventional book to present ideas in a linear fashion. But anyone familiar with reflexive practice will recognize that ideas and insights are often connected in strange ways. Thus, some core ideas in this book are engaged with at multiple points and, sometimes, from legitimately different perspectives. That is in line with the purpose of this book, which is to offer different possible ways of seeing, understanding, developing and applying leader work, rather than suggesting that there is a simple recipe for success. However, I recommend that the best way to engage with the ideas presented in this book in the first instance is still to engage with the chapters in the order presented, since there are some points that build from chapter to chapter. If you choose to join me in this journey, I encourage you to keep in mind the advice of Ramsey (2011), which I have found to be helpful in my own wanderings. He argues that the ideas that we find the most useful can be unexpected and even a little weird, and so we need to be open-minded about the ways that insights come to us. The routes to wisdom may be curious and strange.

Notes

1 Almost everyone changes significantly between their late teens and late 20s (Epstein, 2020). We don't stop changing in later years, but the high school reference point may be an easy one for you to reflect on.

2 Bricolage involves working with the best (and only) tools and materials that we have to hand, acknowledging that this is a creative and improvised response rather than an optimized one.

2

EMBODIMENT AND LEADER WORK

Body talk

Do we pay enough attention to our bodies? Walsh (2021) argues that we have a basic awareness of our bodies and how we relate to them, for example, we adjust our posture to wake or (try to) sleep. He also highlights that we have plenty of expressions that focus on bodily reactions to intense experiences, finding tragedy to be "gut wrenching" or feeling "butterflies in our stomach" when we are nervous. His overall conclusion from his extensive research and practice is that embodiment and embodied skills are core to our humanity. His argument is engaging and persuasive. Yet, research on leadership, and more general studies of management or organization, tend to shy away from direct contact with the body. On a basic level, we recognize our bodies are there and involved in what goes on in our lives and work, but we rarely talk about them. As an example of what happens when we do talk about our bodies, here is a brief story from my experience.[1]

DOI: 10.4324/9781032721507-2

A PERSONAL STORY: SHARED VULNERABILITY

I was leading an important project that would have an impact on our organization's reputation, and there was one colleague on the project team that I really struggled to get on with. John seemed negative, irritable and/or disinterested most of the time, but his experience and input were going to be really important if the project was to work.

One day, we were both first to arrive at the project meeting, which was at the end of a long day. John asked, in the usual formal way, "How are you?". Folk in the United Kingdom know that this is just a greeting, and the acceptable answers are "fine" or "not too bad". For some reason, I actually said how I was feeling:

"Pretty bad. I have something wrong with my leg, I was in pain all night and barely slept. I am exhausted."

"I know how you feel," John replied. "That's how I feel every day. I have chronic insomnia, and my doctor can't seem to do anything about it."

We didn't have a lot more time for conversation then, but a moment of vulnerability, that actually acknowledged how our bodies affect our minds and moods, made for a moment of connection. Just being more aware of John's suffering made it easier to read past the disinterested signals his body was sending in meetings, and helped me to think about being more careful not to schedule pivotal meetings up until the very end of normal office hours. Who else was struggling, in ways that I didn't know?

While there is a lot that we learn when we pay attention to our bodies – and talk about them – research more often deals with how bodies are interpreted and can be a focus for discrimination (Callagher et al., 2021), or considers embodiment in terms that are more abstract and easier to discuss. In particular, there is often attention to the emotions we associate as "coming from" our bodies. For example, Berti, Jarvis, Nikolova and Pitsis (2021) discuss an embodied approach to supporting individuals' development of ethical capabilities – but they equate an "embodied approach" with paying attention to emotions and tacit knowledge. Their work is actually quite useful for guiding the teaching and learning of ethics, but it does a disservice to embodiment to consider the body simply as a vehicle or "black box" for anything that can't be discussed or transferred into explicit knowledge. It is also problematic to assume that embodiment and emotional experiences are *coterminous* – although they do *overlap*, so do emotional experiences and forms of thought (especially for moral emotions: Giner-Sorolla, 2013; Steinbock, 2014). None of this means that we should dismiss the emotional insights we can gather; instead, there is more to say about what is going on with us in relation to our emotions by looking at them *separately*, as we will see in Chapter 3.

Overall, my argument is that, while our emotions and embodied experiences do overlap in some ways, we can get a better understanding of what is going on if we develop a specific focus on each one. In this chapter, I focus on embodiment and its connection to leader work in three sections. The first section considers embodiment and bodily awareness and explains why a micro focus can be helpful. The second section sets out how we can develop our bodily awareness through embodied reflexive practice. The third section, which is followed by a brief summary of the chapter with suggested actions, explains how embodied reflexive practice can inform leader work.

Understanding embodiment and bodily awareness

The emotion-oriented perspective on embodiment taken by Berti et al. (2021) is not uncommon or surprising and, to be fair to them, they are working within (and are consistent with) a particular scholarly tradition. That tradition is clearly rooted in studies that have a more direct focus on emotions (they cite works with this focus, for example, from: Kristjánsson, 2010; Schnall, Haidt, Clore & Jordan, 2008; Tangney, Stuewig & Mashek, 2007). However, the way the body is perceived and discussed in that tradition underlines a more general point. We are often unaware of bodies and relate to them as if they were, somehow, separate from our sense of self – or act as a "black box" from which emotions or thoughts emerge. We usually pay little attention to the body and the physical sensations that go with it until something goes wrong, or pain brings some part into laser-sharp focus.

When we do decide to focus on our bodies (and what it means to have one) we normally end up looking at it through a telescope rather than a microscope, by deploying a bewildering range of social, political and philosophical lenses (Perry & Medina, 2015) that tell us how the body is conceptualized and politicized and not what it is or does, or how we directly experience it (Bigo & Islam, 2022). These lenses serve to separate us from, rather than connect us to, our bodies. The end result is a view of the body as a kind of taxi for our brains (Walsh, 2021) and/or simply a source of emotions (Berti et al., 2021). It is as if a person is the software in a brain's hardware, and the rest of the body is just the system that supplies the power to keep the brain going. But bodies, brains and persons are entwined in more complex ways, and our experiences are almost always embodied. Walsh (2021) is eloquent in his argument on this point: how we live in, and connect with, our bodies is both a reflection of our habits and a means of self-expression. We are all familiar with the idea of body language, and we probably also know that the person slumped in their chair in a meeting might not be communicating disinterest. But as the story at the start of this chapter suggests, there could be something else going on. They could be indicating a lack of attention to their body which has left them with a habitually bad posture, or exhaustion from some physical stress or pain ... or some other cause. And yet, presumptions about that body language and the person's actual embodied state might cause them to be less connected in the meeting. This disconnection might then lead to them missing out on a chance to contribute, or losing an opportunity that they might have valued. The body affects how we think of ourselves and each other, and how we connect.

Thus, in this chapter the focus is on the body and its sensations. Specifically, I wish to address how we experience our bodies, from a reflexive practice perspective. While I tend to take an interpretive and humanistic stance on research in this field, this is an area where careful engagement with the natural sciences is really helpful. The approach of the natural sciences helps us to focus on the micro level and screen out (only temporarily) the wider political and social contexts of bodies to look at them in detail. So, here I encourage you to switch your perspective from the telescope to the microscope. Looking through that apparatus, we find that there are some interesting insights that can open up our thinking about the body, its role in our everyday experiences and how it connects with reflexive practice. The two most interesting themes to focus on are:

Proprioception: our awareness of the physical arrangement of our bodies in space (most people don't need to first identify where their hand is in order to pick up a cup, for example).

Interoception: our awareness, to a greater or lesser extent, of the signals we receive about our bodily functions and states (for example, think about your digestion!).

These themes are interesting because they help us to understand that we can be attuned, more or less effectively, to what is going on in our bodies. I look at each of these themes in more detail at this point.

Arrangement and movement

We are aware of how our body is arranged through *proprioception*. That is, we know the position and action of our body parts and how we are using them without having to look or think about this. For example, if you are running and someone throws you a ball, you don't need to have a conversation with yourself about altering the direction of your run or which hand it would be easiest to catch the ball with. This is pretty basic, but think about what you don't know – what is the position of the middle finger on your left hand, right now? Most people don't have that degree of fine-tuned sensitivity, although specialists who work with body-coaching techniques argue that this can be developed (Walsh, 2021). There are even some arguments that this kind of awareness can be enhanced to include another person, specifically in romantic relationships, and that this "self-overlap" can make relationship bonds stronger. Specifically, Quintard, Jouffe, Hommel and Bouquet (2021) describe how shared bodily experiences can be a source of connection and create a sense of "we-ness" and a feeling of understanding, and being understood by, a partner. This effect is also related to a mirroring of physical habits, along with emotional, social and cognitive influences. It is important to note the overlap with other levels of experience and (implicitly) reflexive practice in this case: no-one is claiming that bodily experiences are the sole mechanism for relationships that support a strong sense of connection with each other. However, Quintard et al. (2021) go some way to explaining why it could be important.

Others have also developed research studies to explore how better awareness (and control of) the body's position, arrangement and action can lead to broader patterns of self-awareness (and therefore reflexive practice). The work of Bigo and Islam (2022) merits particular attention, for its direct focus on the body. They contrast the common focus of studies of embodiment in organizational settings – that tend to look at how bodies are interpreted, depicted and described from a sociological point of view – with their focus on students actually engaged in bodily practice as they explored complex ideas. Their work used a particular approach:

they focused on helping students to develop yoga practice, as a method of supporting embodied learning within a leadership program. They were concerned with how abstract concepts and ideas were understood through (or related to) their participants' experiences and awareness of the postures and intensity of action of different parts of their bodies, as well as how they reflected on their experiences of moving and focusing on their bodies in particular ways. They describe how the meditative forms of bodywork offered by yoga practice allowed their students to approach their learning in a different way. Their study found that leadership students who developed embodied practices gained "conceptual looseness" in relation to learning – and that flexibility in their thinking allowed them to also develop their reflexive practice to challenge emerging understandings. In sum, the ability to be situated in more clearly in (and to be in touch with) the body provided the basis for a different perspective. Others focusing on the body to develop insights in their research processes have reached similar conclusions. For example, Leigh and Brown (2021) argued that the body, being essentially involved during the acquisition of experience, is also involved in the expression of understandings that arise from experience. They also suggest that attention to the body helps to keep the emotional level of understanding alongside thoughtful engagement, rendering our accounts of our experiences more authentic.

Like Bigo and Islam (2022), Leigh and Brown (2021) focused on the body's physical arrangement and movement in their research. On a simple level, these insights are easy for us to understand: perhaps you "sit up straight" when you are paying attention, or "clear your head" through taking a walk, or you have noticed that you are more likely to come up with ideas while taking exercise than while staring at your computer screen. Both Bigo and Islam (2022) and Leigh and Brown (2021) suggest that embodied practices help us not just to develop a greater awareness of the body's position and action, but also to free up the mind to think in new ways. But their insights also suggest that part of this potential for changed awareness comes from a clearer focus on the internal sensations that our bodies produce. There is more going on here than a kind of meditative clarity by guiding the body; instead, there is an invitation to reflexive practice that comes from letting the body guide us. For example, when we say we have a "gut feeling" about what to think or do, that might be more literal than we imagine. How should we attend to and interpret these sensations?

Internal sensations and messages

We all have some level of awareness about what is going on in our bodies, although we don't always pay much attention to the messages the body sends us. Science terms the experience of engaging with these signals *interoception* (Hardy & Hibbert, 2012; Tsakiris & De Preester, 2019), and highlights how such signals can have complex effects on what we think and do. Researchers focusing on interoception help us to understand the complexity that is involved and how the experience can affect us in a number of ways. Berntson, Gianaros and Tsakiris (2019) explain that interoception is complex and multidimensional. In part this is because it involves engaging with *afferent* sensory information that comes from across the body in different ways and from multiple different sources: the sources can include internal organs and bodily systems that we are more or less aware of, but nevertheless have some effect on our emotional perceptions and how we think. The term "afferent" in the description of the experience of interoception roughly means "coming from" – we can think of it as the feedback that we get from the organs and biological systems in our bodies, in response to the signals they receive through the central nervous system or from the outside world. However, not all of the feedback is at a level we can easily capture. For example, some parts of our nervous systems and the chemical messengers (hormones) that regulate our internal organs in our bodies are more closed to us: these systems operate in ways that do not need or allow direct thoughtful attention to their action, but we may infer their involvement *after* a particular experience.

One way in which we begin to have the option to pay attention to what is going on in our bodies is when we have a crisis experience that triggers reflex actions, such as fight-or-flight responses when we face an immediate threat. The body has already decided how to act at such times, but we can moderate that after the fact and choose alternative actions. For example, think about how you might react to hearing a gunshot … and then realizing that it is actually a car engine backfiring. At times when we experience an immediate threat or sense of danger, we might also become more aware of the signals provided by our bodies, experiencing a "sinking feeling" in our abdomen or noticing that our hearts are pounding (with more or less accuracy – Quadt, Critchley & Garfinkel, 2019). Such situations don't have to be life-or-death threats but can instead be the kinds of shock that we encounter in our working lives from time to time. The kind of experiences that Driver (2015) describes – in which we become shocked and angry by discovering some betrayal of trust by an employing organization or our manager – are good examples. In such cases, our bodily systems will lead to a brief fall in our heart rate as the shock of the news affects us, followed by an elevation of the heart rate as we begin to react, the anger kicks in and our sympathetic nervous system guides the body towards action (Hardy & Hibbert, 2012). Not all of the body's systems driving these changes in our bodily state will be open to our attention, but the effects on our heart rate may very well be (Hibbert, 2021a). Perhaps you can remember your heart pounding in a similar situation?

The body's messages, which we notice at particular times, are not unique to threats and crises. Instead, they are amplified versions of the kind of messages that are *always* available to us but normally go unnoticed. But when we pay more attention to bodily sensations, there is a wide range of characteristics that we can distinguish. Walsh (2021) sets out one way of categorizing the characteristics, focusing on five key aspects. The first is concerned with what the bodily sensation is. For example, you would have no trouble distinguishing an itch from a feeling of tightness. The second is concerned with the strength of the feeling: is that itch driving you crazy? The third aspect reflects your disposition towards the experience, that is, whether you find the experience to be pleasant, unpleasant or neutral. Think about, for example, someone gently holding your hand, or plunging your own hand into ice-cold water, or letting it rest in your lap. The fourth aspect is whether the feeling is static or moving. Experiences of digestion can be a good example of the latter. The final aspect is the timing, in the sense of both when the feeling occurred and its duration. Listing these aspects of bodily sensation isn't an agenda for every moment of awareness, but it helps to show us just how much information is on offer.

There are also key technical differences – the categorizations offered by scientists specializing in these areas – between the kinds of information our bodies generate. Specifically, the information that is passed back from our bodies through the central nervous system is grouped into two kinds, based on the source (Berntson, Gianaros & Tsakiris, 2019). One kind of information relates to the signals arising from the structural elements of our bodies – our skin, muscles, joints and so on – and that is described as somatic.[2] The other types of signal are those that come from our tissues and internal organs, including the information we get from our senses of taste and smell, and such information is described as visceral.[3] Our ability to engage with the different kinds of somatic and visceral information can vary, in three ways (Van den Bergh, Zacharioudakis & Petersen, 2019, especially p212). First, we can vary in our "interoceptive sensibility", which is our attitude in relation to the available sensations of our internal bodily processes. That is, do we tend to pay attention to what is going on in our bodies, or do we overlook this? Second, variations in our "interoceptive accuracy and sensitivity" also exist. These linked characteristics reflect how accurate and precise we are when we pay attention to the signals of what is going on in our bodies. For example, many of us might know if our heart is racing but we could not say precisely how fast. In contrast, Walsh (2021) explains that he is able to count his heart rate without feeling his pulse, since he has learned to focus on the signals that are already present in parts of the body. Third, there is "interoceptive awareness", which relates to the overall connections between the previous two abilities, through which we can have more or less confidence about what signals our body is generating and how to accurately describe them.

Background effects and diversity

We will return later to awareness of our bodies, in relation to both knowing the arrangement and movement of the body and engagement with the internal sensations that come from it. But at this point we need to explore what is going on when we are *unaware* of such signals, or when the signals are disrupted. Some of these effects have come to light when individuals have undergone nerve surgery that has had unforeseen and complex side effects. For example, Berntson et al. (2019) discuss the effects, on a particular patient, of nerve surgery they receive to control their excessive sweating. This kind of surgery disrupts signals both from and to the central nervous system: nerves provide for "two-way traffic" and the surgery "cuts off both lanes". This means that to turn off the *outward* signals to disrupt the excessive sweating, a side effect is the disruption of *inward* signals through interoception. The effects on the emotion experienced by the patient were profound and unexpected. She described the changes she experienced in enlightening and striking ways. For her, the changes included the expected control of physical symptoms but also changes in how she experienced emotions and controlled her behavior. Her emotions felt more "blunt" and she felt she was less concerned with everyday situations and lacked fear. She also felt that her behaviors were less inhibited and her self-control diminished. Overall, her conclusion was that even her personality had significantly changed as a side effect of the surgery.

Insights about the links between our nervous systems and our emotions, thoughts and behaviors are also validated by the experience of those who are neurodivergent. They can experience their bodies as part of themselves in quite different ways. In this vein, Higashida (2013) has written – in a way that is really enlightening for those of us who struggle to understand – about his experience of autism. He describes how signals that others may wish to pick up on are not easily shared by him, leading to false assumptions about the bodily state of people with autism. A good example concerns how he deals with pain, which explains why some people with autism might not show signs of physical pain. He describes how he finds it so difficult to express how his body is feeling that it seems easier to behave as if the pain is gone, rather than letting people know about it. Higashida (2013) also goes on to explain how, despite its characterization as a developmental disorder associated with the brain, he does not experience autism in that way. Instead, his account of autism is very closely connected to his understanding of his body, and his experiences of how that relates to his thoughts and emotions. His belief is that his nervous system is working effectively, but all of his attention can become focused on one part of his body, leading to the impression that something is seriously wrong.

Capturing insights from bodily awareness

The examples above show why the signals in and about our bodies can be important on fundamental levels that we don't necessarily realize. These signals can affect our experience of emotions *and* how we think. This insight goes some way to explaining why coaches and therapists will use bodywork to help people address emotional concerns and still their thoughts (Harris, 2019; Walsh, 2021).

Going further, we can see that there are potential benefits in understanding and connecting with our bodies – if we can – before trying to work through difficult thoughts and emotions. Walsh (2021) argues that we can improve the accuracy of our bodily awareness through practice. The insights of others confirm that there are reasons why it could be helpful to do so. For example, Quadt et al. (2019) found that a poor level of awareness of our own emotional state and that of other people (a condition known as alexythimia) was associated with poor interoceptive accuracy, which aligns with the insights offered by Higashida (2013) and Berntson et al. (2019) mentioned earlier. In addition, there is potential for all of us to experience how incidents that affect the body can work through our emotions and thoughts to have an effect on the sense we make of what is going on around us. This has been illustrated by Hardy and Hibbert (2012 pp15–16), through reflecting on a classic experiment conducted by Dutton and Aron (1974):

> Schachter and Singer's two-factor theory of emotion suggests that individuals interpret their physiological states in the light of the cues available to them (Schachter & Singer, 1962). This was demonstrated by Dutton and Aron who looked at the behavior of men who had just crossed a rather frightening 450' long cable suspension bridge over Capilano Canyon in Vancouver, which had a tendency to sway, tilt and wobble, potentially allowing the individual to fall over the low handrails to the rocks 230' below. These men were compared with men who had crossed a stout cedar bridge which was only 10' above a small shallow rivulet. In each case the men were interviewed by an attractive female researcher and the dependent variable was the number telephoning the lab to speak with her further for more information. 9/18 of the participants crossing the wobbly suspension bridge telephoned the lab whereas only 2/16 of those crossing the firm control bridge did so (for a male control interviewer the figures were 1/6 and 2/7 respectively) (Dutton & Aron, 1974). The authors speculated that the men were psychologically and physiologically aroused by crossing the bridge and misattributed this arousal as attraction to the female researcher, hence the increased number of telephone calls. Effectively these individuals were likely to have physiological signs of arousal, such as elevated heart rate, which they interocepted. They then interpreted this as being due to the presence of the attractive researcher rather than the bridge they had just crossed. Hence their interoception altered their psychological state.

Understanding our bodily signals better is not necessarily something that we can bolster with a technological solution, if we remain inattentive to the context of our experiences. Instead, we need to think about the interoceptive experience and the context together. In earlier work (Hibbert, 2021a), I described how a health scare led me to be anxious about my heart rate and needed to have a battery of medical tests. While waiting for the test results, by paying close attention to my heart rate I managed to create a worryingly high count just through the combination of anxiety and hypervigilance … and the possession of a smart watch that allowed me to constantly monitor my pulse. After all of the formal medical test results came in, my original health scare proved to be something much less serious than I had feared, much like the one associated with my later anxiety. At the time, however, I did not know that the "real" problem was relatively trivial – and it is remarkable how much attention you can devote to an apparently worrying symptom in a short time. But this also points to another important aspect of interoception and its effects: our experience of time. Episodes of pain or stress can feel much longer than calm, stress- and pain-free periods, and this effect can work in combination with the effect of emotions on our overall sense of time (Wittman & Meissner, 2019).

Overall, attention to our bodies is not always easy or trouble free, and we may radically misinterpret the signals that we become aware of. To balance the negative effects of conditions, contexts and situations which diminish the value of interoception, there are positive effects from developing a better awareness of our bodily sensations. Critchley and Harrison (2013) suggest that better awareness can be connected to both improvements in the richness of our emotional experiences and help us to be more effective when we need to regulate our emotions. To put it another way, there is an important dynamic between having an accurate sense of what is going on in the world around us and a good awareness of what is going on within our bodies. This dynamic affects the way in which we feel "at home" in our bodies and the world (Allen & Tsakaris, 2019; Gallagher, 2000). If we feel "more at home" in this way, it leads to two important benefits (Babo-Rebelo & Tallon-Baudry, 2019; Berntson et al., 2019; Fotopolou & Tsakiris, 2017): we are likely to have a more stable sense of self than we otherwise might; and being "at home" in, and more aware of, our bodies also helps us to be more aware of others. These benefits that come with better awareness of our bodies can be developed and captured through embodied reflexive practice.

Embodied reflexive practice

Reflexive practice is concerned with having a better sense of awareness, and questioning what is happening in the situations we encounter, in order to change how we act and think. This clearly needs to include attention to what is going on in our bodies. As I mentioned at the start of the chapter, we tend to overlook both proprioception (an awareness of the body's position, arrangement and action) and interoception (the signals within our bodies). Leder (2019) has argued that all of that information is often considered to be less significant than rational thought, despite the important effects and possibilities afforded by embodied experience – which are many. For example, interoceptive awareness has some bearing on: the richness and form of our emotions, as well as how we regulate them (Berntson et al., 2019; Critchley & Harrison, 2013); the stability of our sense of self-awareness along with our ability to be aware of the bodily and emotional states of others (Berntson et al., 2019; Fotopolou & Tsakiris, 2017; Quadt et al., 2019); and even our sense of time (Wittman & Meissner, 2019).

Clearly, we navigate our social world in and through our bodies, and how our bodies respond to the situations we encounter will influence and shape how we behave and adapt. This shaping happens through direct effects on bodily processes, as well through the ways that embodied experiences contribute to the pattern of our emotions and thoughts. Cultivating reflexive practice focused on bodily awareness can allow us to be more aware of these effects and so provide a more stable sense of self in amongst all of these shaping and patterning effects. So, we need to develop forms of practice that support an "interoceptive sensibility" or a willingness to pay attention to these signals, and in time to become more accurate and precise in interpreting them (Van den Bergh et al., 2019). In this part of the chapter, I explore reflexive practices that can help us with that quest, in order to connect with later insights about what this looks like in leader work.

The works cited in this section are drawn from a range of sources that include leadership development texts, descriptions of bodywork (notably yoga) and meditative traditions. It is important to emphasize, at this point, that it is beyond the scope of the book to offer training in formal techniques and traditions (such as bodywork and yoga) and you should seek such training elsewhere if you want to develop that aspect of your practice in greater depth. Instead, in the text that follows, my intention is to offer you a "way in" that helps you consider how particular approaches may be useful for reflexive practice.

Developing awareness of the body

If our goal is to have a better understanding of the signals within our body, we need to do so in ways that connect with the types of bodily awareness that are available to us. This means that embodied reflexive practice needs to connect with what is happening within the body and with how our body moves or is arranged (Küpers & Pauleen, 2015). These kinds of practices can be learned best and are most effective when they are engaged with regularly, or become habits, and typically involve focused movement exercises such as yoga (Bigo & Islam, 2022) or techniques for focused attention such as mindfulness meditation (Rigg, 2018; Williams & Penman, 2011). Of course, there is a lot more to both yoga and mindfulness than the practices I focus on here, where my scope is necessarily limited.

Mindfulness includes a simple technique for enhancing our awareness of our bodies through the "body scan" meditation described by Williams and Penman (2011). The ideas behind this practice are concordant with many other forms of body coaching (Walsh, 2021) and therapeutic interventions for emotional stress (Harris, 2019), as we will see later. However, in the form I am considering here, the body scan is simply a calm and orderly movement of our attention around our body, while in a relaxed position (lying down is normally recommended). As someone who does not have a consistent meditation practice I still find the body scan (and mindful movement) to be useful, but not necessarily easy to do. The body scan is about paying attention to what is going on in the body with interest and without judgment, but like everyone who does not meditate regularly I get distracted by a wandering mind and/or get too relaxed and fall asleep! Nevertheless, I have found this kind of practice worthwhile and helpful. The overall idea is that you can be more at home in your body, but also note – without alarm – the messages that show you that there may be things that you need to be aware of. It is important to note here that mindfulness practices work best within an overall program, require some commitment to (and understanding of) meditation and are not for everyone. If you feel that it might be right for you, there is further guidance and a link to a guided body scan available on the internet in the "Summary and actions" section at the end of this chapter. For all of us who strive to be re-flexive practitioners, who know that the body affects and interacts with our emotions and thoughts (Berntson et al., 2019; Critchley & Harrison, 2013; Quadt et al., 2019), this level of focused attention is essential. It is important to note that the body scan meditation is, obviously, not something that we can engage in constantly. The body scan requires relaxation and focused attention and sits best within an encompassing practice of meditation: it is difficult to pay gentle and curious attention to parts of your body in turn, especially if you have a "wandering mind" like I so often do. But, through engaging with this practice, we can become more familiar with our bod-ies and their signals, allowing us to notice changes and adapt more easily when they occur. That adaptation might involve us correcting issues with our bodies (thinking about our posture, state of tiredness and so on, for example) or being alert to how the effects of our bodies on our emotions and thoughts are playing out.

Working with the body to allow awareness on other levels

Paying attention to the body when we have time and space for relaxed attention – as in the example of the body scan meditation above – is not always possible. In particular, there can be times when emotions are over-whelming and we find it difficult to process what is going on and feel we need to suppress our attention rather than engage with the problem at hand (Hibbert, Beech et al., 2022). We might still notice some bodily signals at such times – maybe some tightness in the gut, a general sense of contrac-tion, changes in the heart rate and so on – but they are associated with the body being an "amplifier" of suffering (Williams & Penman, 2011) rather than our "safe home". Attention to the body can still help us at such times, but we need to approach it in a different way, so that we can deal with what is going on in our unsettled condition. Using our bodies in this way is described by the influential therapist and trainer Harris (2019), metaphori-cally, as "dropping anchor": a way of finding safety in a storm. One of the exercises that he offers to accomplish this is the ACE exercise. I summarize my approach to his exercise in this way:

Acknowledging our present experience, including our thoughts, emotions and physical sensations. Harris (2019) suggests that you might want to put this into words, perhaps even speaking aloud what you are feeling.

Alternatively, I have sometimes used (very brief) free writing for this, which has the benefit (for me) of being a practice which leads me naturally into the second step.

Coming back into the body, by using it. Harris (2019) suggests you might do that by, for example, getting up and moving around, changing your posture or paying attention to and controlling your breathing (you might wish to look at mindfulness practices in connection with that option – see Williams & Penman, 2011).

Engaging with the world around you, by using all of your five senses. Harris (2019) explains that this helps to establish that there is more going on than the emotions or thoughts that may be troubling you. Once you have established that, you can think about where your attention would be most helpful.

I find Harris' (2019) dropping anchor exercise very easy to use informally in a number of ways and situations, even when I am not necessarily experiencing *deep* suffering. For example, I might be working on a difficult and emotionally charged email exchange at home, announce to myself that there is a tightness and pain in my shoulders and that I am tired and anxious. I get up and go to the kitchen to wash the dishes. At my kitchen window I can see the bees making the flowers twitch in the garden, in dappled sunshine that filters through the trees, in the trees that stir in the breeze I can hear whispering, beyond the window. The clean lemon smell of the dish detergent rises up from the warm water flowing gently over my hands, and I feel my shoulders loosening. I am ready to think about the tricky challenge that I need to address.

The ACE exercise (or something similar to it) is also something you may experience if you are working with a therapist, which leads me to an important point. If you find yourself in persistent emotional distress that is difficult for you to handle, then it would be wise to seek professional help. I am not a therapist, and this book is not a source of therapeutic advice. However, the fact that something has a therapeutic origin does not mean that it is "not for you" if you don't need expert help. Many of us (including me) have found that the lessons we learned from professionals are useful in everyday life as part of our ongoing reflexive practice. Moreover, all of us have plenty of "ordinary" stress and distress to handle and benefit from finding ways to manage it. For that reason, the "Summary and actions" section at the end of this chapter includes a link to a practitioner's example of how they use the ACE exercise.

In addition to its particular benefits for handling distress, the ACE exercise alerts us to the other kind of bodily awareness that we touched on earlier, namely an awareness of the body's position, action and movement. It shows us how movement and attention can bring us back into the body and allow us to pay more attention to what is going on. As mentioned earlier in this chapter, recent work on using yoga in leadership programs has built on this idea, to support new ways of engaging with issues and concepts that have a bearing on how leadership is understood. Bigo and Islam (2022) describe how the yoga practices they used in their leadership class helped students in three ways. First, it helped their students on the most basic level to be more centered and "at home" in their bodies, through a range of practices including breathing exercises, relaxation techniques and forms of meditation. Second – and facilitated by the philosophical aspects of yoga as well as the practical techniques – their students became more comfortable in accepting the ambiguity and uncertainty that was part of their everyday experience. Third, the relatively accepting environment that was created in this way helped their students to work out their leadership ideas in ways that were more open and reflective than they otherwise might have been.

Similar approaches to bodily attention and bodily learning (Yakhlef, 2010) can also be developed from mindfulness techniques and provide a similar basis for generating openness to uncertainty and supporting reflection (Rigg, 2018). In part, mindfulness provides an alternative to yoga for bodily practices because mindfulness approaches can also incorporate or involve particular practices focused on mindful movement (Williams & Penman, 2011). Simple mindful movements may also be an easier starting point than yoga for two reasons – because they are less physically demanding, and because they do not have such a broad philosophical context to engage with (although it does have a clear Buddhist background, the spiritual hinterland of mindfulness is much less apparent in many approaches).

Embodied reflexive practice and leader work

If we have developed reflexive practice to include attention to bodily signals and have ways of recovering from emotional distress through "coming back to the body", then we are in a position to think about what that could mean for the development of our leader work. There are two main areas to focus on in relation to that. The first is to think about the kinds of practice we might use in the contexts of leader work, to be more at home in our bodies and better able to engage with others. The second is what the overall outcome of reflexive practice focused on bodily awareness might be, for how we are perceived and received by others when we engage in leader work.

The main practice I would like to suggest, which builds on insights from mindfulness (Rigg, 2018; Williams & Penman, 2011) and yoga (Bigo & Islam, 2022), is centering. This has some similarities to the ACE exercise (Harris, 2019) that I discussed earlier, but instead of being about handling overwhelming emotions and distress it is about a gentler restoration of balance, poise and readiness to engage. Walsh (2021) explains that centering is a way of paying attention to and adapting our posture and sense of balance to present our "best self". He explains that the everyday stress and distress of organizational life means that people are rarely able to manage their physical state, and he offers a simple ABC technique to help people to address this problem. My engagement with this technique varies slightly from the details of his approach on some points, and involves:

Awareness: paying attention, as much as you are able, to your body and the sensations you experience through it in the moment. This attention includes all of your five senses, as well as giving some attention to your breathing. It is difficult to do that all at once, and I find it easiest to first pay attention to touch, noticing where I am supported on a chair (or through my feet if standing), then to run through smell, taste and hearing before turning to sight (which otherwise dominates sensory impressions for me).

Balance and relaxation: try to achieve, without great effort, a balanced posture so that you feel you are centered left and right, front and back: the end goal is to feel relaxed but in a dignified way, rather than slumping, and it starts with attention to your posture. (Walsh (2021) also suggests imagining a light emanating from you in all directions equally, but I find this difficult and not essential.) When you feel you have a balanced and dignified posture, try to relax from the head progressively downwards to your abdomen, breathing deeply when you are done.

Connection: call to mind people with whom you share mutual care and respect. Walsh (2021) suggests two alternative sources of connection that you could try: (1) looking for connected people who are in the present context with you, rather than calling them to mind, but I find that distracting; or (2) using some mental image as a link to your values, but I have not found an image that works effectively for me.

Importantly, compared to Walsh's (2021) original approach, I combine Balance and Core relaxation (the original "C" in Walsh's version), adopting his optional "extra" C of connection as a more important focus in the way I use this. Nevertheless, despite its possible variations, you will notice that the ABC technique has similarities and differences to Harris' (2019) ACE technique, and in both cases there are ways that you can adapt the practices to help them work best for you. The most important difference with Walsh's (2021) ABC approach is that it is not going to be helpful if you are suffering from intrusive or overwhelming emotions, which would need to be acknowledged first. But the ABC approach is simple and quick to engage with, and it can be used in situations when stress or tension has been ratcheting up but is not overwhelming.

Because stress and tension play out in your body in ways that are obvious to others (Palmer & Crawford, 2013), using a centering technique (like ABC or some other approach) as part of your reflexive practice may have an influence on others. In this way, using centering may very well help others to be at ease, too. This effect is possible because most of us do not have a complex vocabulary to describe body language, but we instinctively read cues from how people hold themselves and use their body positioning to engage with us – or avoid engagement. Importantly, the messages our bodies send may be at odds with our *deliberate* intentions but will be interpreted by others without any need for direct thought. Palmer and Crawford (2013) explain that this is tied to the normal human capacity to have a "theory of mind". This involves intuitively processing non-verbal signals alongside the things that people say, to reach conclusions about their internal state. This is part of the reason that a centering exercise like Walsh's (2021) ABC technique can be helpful, since it will likely give you an upright and dignified posture through the achievement of balance – and that posture will likely be interpreted (subconsciously) as conveying confidence, as opposed to a slumped posture indicating defeat (Palmer & Crawford, 2013).

Importantly, Palmer and Crawford (2013) are not suggesting that body language can be used in a manipulative or persuasive way. Instead, they explain how the messages we are deliberately trying to send will not have the effect we expect if our body is saying something different, and that trying to "cover up" parts of ourselves is exhausting and ineffective. This is why it is so important to think about building up our bodily awareness through techniques like the body scan (Williams & Penman, 2011) and having (perhaps a repertoire of) techniques like "dropping anchor" (Harris, 2019) and centering (Walsh, 2021) that help us to be our best, balanced selves when we most need to be. Overall, instead of seeking dishonest influence, the goal is *congruence* – an alignment between our deliberate intentions and the way we feel and express that in our bodies. Palmer and Crawford (2013) argue that it is difficult (and perhaps exhausting) to have a physical stance that is at odds with the thoughts and feelings we are trying to convey; they describe this as an attempt to cover up parts of ourselves that ends up with "leaking incongruence" that is obvious to those around us. If you have ever tried to seem engaged and positive through a really depressing and protracted meeting or when you are in pain, you will know exactly what they mean.

Palmer and Crawford (2013) go on to argue that others have the ability to detect our incongruence, through spotting a "mixed message". They suggest that when we notice that kind of signal, we are much less likely to trust the spoken message when the body language is at odds with it. This is an important point when thinking about leader work, but it also raises some issues for us to think about when people are simply not able to present themselves in a congruent way. That might be because they are carrying a burden of enduring suffering like grief (Kivenen, 2021), or because they have a difference, like autism, which means that they cannot easily communicate their inner state in ways that we can understand (Higashida, 2013). In either case, incongruence does not mean that their body is indicating that their internal state is at odds with (or not genuinely aligned with) their intentions, but that something more fundamental or difficult is going on for them. It may be a good idea to find time for a quiet and supportive conversation, if the incongruence is persistent, while respecting that people will choose their own boundaries about what they wish to share with us and allowing for that. These are important reflections for us in considering our own leader work and how we judge that of others, and how we create a culture that enables people to be fully themselves in their work (Zak & Winn, 2016). If we can do that, we have good reason to be optimistic about the benefits that attention to embodiment can bring, not least feeling that our body is our true home (Walsh, 2021).

Summary and actions

In this chapter I have explained how the different kinds of signals we experience in our bodies have important effects on the way our emotions are experienced, how our thoughts take shape and influence how we interact with and understand other people. Based on those understandings, I have set out the kinds of reflexive practice that can help us to improve our bodily awareness and – in due course – form a constituent part of our leader work. If you are looking for ways to begin applying these insights in leader work, you will find suggestions below.

Take care of yourself

Any practice that involves focusing on the body (and related emotions) may not be suitable for everyone, especially if you are carrying trauma. If you feel distress when trying to engage with such practices or are in any doubt, stop and seek professional guidance. There is absolutely no shame in seeking help.

Develop bodily awareness as part of your reflexive practice

This might involve simple techniques like the body scan (described earlier in the chapter) but it would be most helpful if it was within the context of a program. For example, Williams and Penman's (2011) book can be used at home, or you might wish to take up a short mindfulness course if that feels appropriate for you. Alternatively, you will find many resources available on the internet that you can explore. If you do this, try to look for a recognized practitioner: with that in mind, there is a guided body scan from Jon Kabat Zinn (a leading mindfulness expert) available at: www.youtube.com/watch?v=_DTmGtznab4. But don't worry if formal techniques or practices are not for you – they are not helpful for everyone. Just being aware that your body has messages for you, and trying to pay attention to that, may be enough.

Use centering when the need arises

Once you have developed your bodily awareness it will be easier to use techniques like Walsh's (2021) ABC approach to centering. This will help you engage in an open and balanced way with others and avoid some of the issues of offering incongruent body language that means you offer "mixed messages". If you would find it helpful, you can find a very short video of Mark Walsh explaining the ABC technique here: www.youtube.com/watch?v=wsXHcDBcuEI. Alternatively, if you would like to find out more about "dropping anchor" through using the ACE approach (Harris, 2019) instead, you can find an overview which has been produced by a team at the Leeds NHS Trust here: www.leedsth.nhs.uk/assets/7c353df422/Dropping-Anchor-Russ-Harris-Infographic-.pdf.

Think about congruence generously

Some people may not be able to offer congruent body language and you will need to think about how you can allow for that. For those that can adapt, however, you can help them "come back to the body", perhaps by taking a break and stretching, or going for a walk if the context of leader work allows for that.

Notes

1 I have adapted this slightly to present an honest account of my learning while protecting the identity of the other person.
2 This just means related to your body in general, rather than being related to your mind.
3 Literally related to the viscera – the main internal organs of the body.

3

EMOTIONS AND LEADER WORK

What emotions do

Emotions can be triggered rapidly and catch you unawares, influencing your actions before you have the chance to think about what is going on – or what to do about it. Our emotions provide important information about what is going on within and around us, and form a faster "information system" than the thoughts that follow (Immordino-Yang, 2016). You don't have to think about, for example, getting angry or experiencing fear. You cannot stop these fast reactions, but you can become more aware of them and develop different choices. Sometimes that involves holding onto your emotions, or helping others to deal with theirs, as I explain in the following story.

A PERSONAL STORY: PERMISSION TO GRIEVE

For a time, I covered the role of Vice-Principal for Education. It was a large portfolio, which covered not just education but also other areas,

---

DOI: 10.4324/9781032721507-3

including student services and the chaplaincy. So when we lost a student to suicide, there was a lot that I needed to focus on: making sure that the frontline staff handling the grief of students and staff, and setting up counselling, were OK; ensuring that our processes and intervention teams were reviewed for any lessons that we could learn; and keeping people engaged in suicide awareness campaigns when people don't like to talk about or consider it.

I got on with what needed to be done but it was hard: I loved our wonderful students and I felt like my heart was being ripped out. Holding back my own grief was agony.

Once the initial crisis response was under way and there was a chance to catch a breath, there was a knock on my office door. It was my old boss, who had managed the portfolio before me. She didn't really have to say anything – from the moment I saw her come through the door I knew that she got it, and that she was there for me. She just quietly closed the door and sat with me while I let it all out, howling and sobbing, until I was ready to carry on. I think I would have broken without her providing me the space to grieve. I later recognized how this was not just a moment of genuine compassion, but also a powerful example of leader work on her part.

In this chapter, I focus on emotions and their connection to leader work in three sections. The first section considers and explains emotions and how they affect us, with an extensive focus on moral emotions since these are the most complex in their nature and effects. The second section sets out how we can develop our awareness through emotional reflexive practice. The third main section explains how emotional reflexive practice can inform leader work. The main sections are followed by a brief summary of the chapter and potential ideas for implementation.

Can you feel it? Understanding emotions and their effects

Becoming more aware of our emotions is important even though, in our organizational lives, we may have been encouraged to see emotions as an illogical distraction. Indeed, in organizations emotions are generally seen to be sources of disruption that require regulation and suppression (Tee, 2015; Troth, Lawrence, Jordan & Ashkanasy, 2018). But against that, there are emerging arguments that emotions provide energy for action and can also act as a useful signal, drawing our attention to salient information about why the emotion was evoked in the first place (Geddes, Callister & Gibson, 2020; Lindebaum & Gabriel, 2016).

Emotions are, in any case, important in shaping how we think about ourselves in different situations, and whether we feel that the identity we are presenting in the moment is coherent (Sela-Sheffy & Leshem, 2016). Perhaps you have been stressed, edgy and short-tempered at the end of a difficult day, and feel that you are "not yourself"? On the flip side, when our identity work – the ways we seek to be recognized by others in a certain way[1] – is threatened or challenged, that is likely to lead to difficult emotional experiences (Callagher et al., 2021). When emotions are so tied to our sense of who we are, it is not possible to strip them out from our everyday experience, whatever the norms might be in the places we find ourselves. Indeed, Burkitt (2012) argues that our thoughts are always formed in the context of emotion, and what we feel about the world and the people around us is likely to influence what we think of them.

Are emotions are always involved in experience?

In contrast to Burkitt (2012), Mills and Kleinman (1988) earlier argued that when we are involved in doing something that is routine and habitual, or where we have deliberately tried to develop some kind of "rational detachment", we may be in a neutral emotional state. It is easy to think, however, of examples where we engage with other people in routine contexts where this might not be true. Have you ever noticed that a shop worker is sad, and caught their mood? Do your own emotions show in your everyday work life? For most of us there is some emotional spillover, and we can also find deep emotional experiences and attachments forming in the middle of situations where we are trying hard to be "professional" (Hibbert, 2021a). Even for those professions and situations where we might imagine emotional detachment must be developed – from the military to medicine – there is evidence that it is not so; those involved in those professions can be deeply affected by their emotions at the time of an experience, and potentially for a long time afterwards (Hibbert, 2021b; Laing & Moules, 2014).

So, while the notion of professional detachment may discourage us from talking or writing about our emotions (Gilmore & Kenny, 2015), they are still there. Emotions are central to how we focus on and engage with people, how we begin to understand what is going on around us and whether we care about this knowledge (Gray, 2008). Emotions are thus important in shaping our actions and possibilities for finding meaning in our life with others, from everyday interactions to the most difficult of circumstances (Hibbert et al., 2019). For example, Brown and de Graaf (2013) found that emotions were central to how terminal cancer patients made purposeful plans for their remaining time. They describe how the entanglement of thoughts and emotions, for the patients they worked with, were strongly influenced by the presence or absence of hope. Hope is a complex emotion, that reflects our expectations about our life with others in the future. The hope that some of Brown and de Graaf's (2013) terminal cancer patients experienced was not delusional (they knew they had little time to live) but instead focused on crafting meaningful time with those they loved, in whatever way was possible.

Emotions and time

It will be obvious to you that emotions are not just concerned with everyday here-and-now experiences. The work of Brown and de Graaf (2013) cited above, for example, has shown how emotions can be involved in connecting our present and our future possibilities; they have a role in our qualitative experience of time. Similarly, emotions are evoked through memory, in relation to powerful experiences that have left a lasting impression on us. An experience of the power of emotions in our memories is shared in the work of Hibbert, Mavin and Beech (2022, p7):

> I have long felt that I have not achieved enough and haven't worked hard enough, and I now relate that to not having done enough to win my father's approval. When I allow myself to think about him I mainly feel sad and upset.
>
> He died suddenly and unexpectedly. At the time, I was doing my PhD which turned out fine and I passed two years later but, although I like graduations, I couldn't bring myself to respond to the university invitations and didn't go to my own graduation. When my father died people said: "you're the head of the family now, you'll have to come

back home". I didn't feel anywhere near being a head of a family, I felt ripped apart and I didn't go "home".

At the utmost level of impact, both intense and damaging experiences and chronic suffering can have a lasting effect, to the extent that we experience ongoing trauma and emotional pain. Reflecting on the difficult experiences we have all shared in recent years suggests that we may need to be more aware of this possibility. Times of war, pandemic and severe economic crisis have affected people across the globe, leading to the potential for many of us to carry some form of psychological trauma, as individuals or as members of organizations in social contexts that have been severely disrupted. There is a real possibility that many of us have experienced some post-traumatic stress that we need to address (Greenberg & Hibbert, 2020; Maitlis, 2020; Tedeschi, Shakespeare-Finch, Taku & Calhoun; Van der Kolk, 2015). It is important for me to remind you, at this point, that if you feel that you may be experiencing post-traumatic stress, or other emotional struggles which have a significant impact on you, then you would probably benefit from skilled, professional help. I emphasize: I am not offering medical or therapeutic advice in this book and reflexive practice is not therapy. Indeed, reflexive practice is not going to be helpful for you if therapy is what you need – even if it can still help your leader work. But that reminder allows me to suggest that there is only one kind of emotion you should pay no attention to: any sense of shame in asking for help.

We may not all have experienced emotional trauma to the extent that we have post-traumatic stress. However, we can still experience an "emotional imprint" from difficult experiences even if these do not reach the levels that might qualify for a trauma diagnosis or lead us to seek professional help. In particular, we may feel the need to "contain" powerful emotional experiences, especially if they are negative, but that leaves us with unresolved emotion work (Hochschild, 1979) to do in processing the experience at a later date (Hibbert, Beech et al., 2022). That process may involve both a re-engagement with a personally significant emotional experience and accepting it as meaningful (Corlett, 2013; Evans, Ribbens McCarthy, Bowlby, Wouangoa & Kébé, 2017), while also trying to gain some critical distance from the experience in order to examine it. I will return to how we go about handling this "postponed emotion work", and benefit from the understanding that flows from it, a little later in the chapter. First, in order to engage with our emotions, it is helpful to understand that they can be of different kinds, the most complex of which are moral emotions.

Complex forms: moral emotions

Emotions span a range from the more direct and *basic* forms (like fear or anger) to more complex *moral* emotions like shame, guilt or pride, among many others (Steinbock, 2014). The difference between basic and moral emotions is that the latter are concerned with what we feel is right or wrong in our life with others, and influence how we behave in social contexts because of that (Giner-Soralla, 2013). To help distinguish the types, Figure 3.1 provides a summary of the characteristics of basic and moral emotions.

When we experience moral emotions we are still guided by a more rapid system than deliberative thought, but that rapid response is informed by what we know through learning how to go about our lives in particular social contexts. For example, imagine you believe that you are the only person in a room when you accidentally break a vase … and then you notice that you are not the only person in the room. Yikes! You may well feel shame, and blush, without having to think about the social rules that apply to a simple accident. Those rules were absorbed some time ago, to the extent you may not even need other people to be present to experience moral emotions. Moral emotions – guilt, shame, pride and so on – are therefore experienced individually but are social by definition (shame, for example, makes no sense without (at least implicit) observers). We adjust and control our behavior in relation to what is perceived to be appropriate or inappropriate in a given social situation through these kinds of emotional

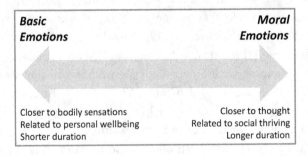

Figure 3.1 The characteristics of basic and moral emotions

experiences. Moral emotional experiences can, therefore, also be positive. For example, *admiration* of another person for their virtue is a positive moral emotion, which can both increase our attention to that person and motivate us towards positive actions that are modeled on theirs (Immordino-Yang, 2016).

In addition to having both positive and negative forms, there can also be blurred boundaries between some basic and moral emotions, depending on the situation. Such blurred boundaries are especially apparent in the case of anger (Lindebaum & Gabriel, 2016; Warren, Sekhon, Winkelman & Waldrop, 2022). For example, if you see someone mistreating a colleague or friend you may well get angry, even though the mistreatment is not directed against you personally – your response is based on the social rules that you have absorbed, and this is *moral anger* or indignation, focused on what is right or wrong at the social level. So, it can be difficult to decide how to categorize emotions or set the boundaries on a particular level. Because of this, if you look at emotions one way they can resemble (or be closely connected to) embodied, physiological processes. However, if you look at emotions another way then they are much more closely connected to processes of thought that we have picked up unconsciously, through learning social rules (Immordino-Yang, 2016).

Perhaps because of their complexity, moral emotions have been characterized and catalogued in a number of ways. However, classifications tend to focus on one or more of three aspects (Dasborough, Hannah & Zhu, 2020; Körner, Tscharaktschiew, Schindler, Schulz & Rudolph, 2016; Steinbock, 2014). The first aspect is their *positive or negative valence*: do we like or loathe the experience of a particular moral emotion? The second aspect is the *individual impact*: how does a particular moral emotion affect the experiences and actions of a person triggering, experiencing or observing it? The third aspect is the *social impact*: how do we understand ourselves *in relation to others* and learn and adapt in response to moral emotions?

Körner et al. (2016) focus largely on valence and social aspects, and describe positive moral emotions (admiration, pride, respect), negative moral emotions (anger, indignation, contempt) and discordant moral emotions (sympathy, schadenfreude). In the case of discordant moral emotions, a person experiencing the emotion and a person observing it will categorize it in opposite ways – schadenfreude is an example of this experience, when a positive emotional experience can be based on observing someone else experiencing negative emotions. Imagine, for example, if you have a rival who is publicly shamed for some transgression, and you take quiet pleasure in seeing them put in their place. In contrast, Dasborough et al. (2020) focus directly on the individual effects of moral emotions on how they suppress or lead to action, separating moral emotions such as guilt and shame, which discourage certain actions, from those like sympathy, compassion and pride, which have the opposite effect by encouraging action. Distinctively, Steinbock's (2014) treatment of moral emotions establishes three categories in a different way, focused on whether they draw attention to ourselves in the present moment (emotions of self-givenness, such as shame), focus on our future possibilities (moral emotions of possibility, such as hope) or draw our attention to others as the foundation of our social thriving (moral emotions of otherness, such as trusting).

Functions of moral emotions and functional conflicts

As the variety of categorizations shows, there is clearly a lot going on in connection with moral emotions. Giner-Sorolla (2018) explains how to unpick this complexity to see how they lead to particular effects, through paying attention to the fact that moral emotions have a range of different functions that can help us thrive in social groups, but the functions cannot all be executed equally effectively at the same time. Giner-Sorolla's (2013, 2018) functional conflict theory helps to understand what can happen when the "wrong" function of a moral emotion is triggered. The theory first identifies and characterizes four different functions of moral emotions, each of which I explain here. First, they form a key part of a motivated appraisal system that leads to adaptive behavior. That is, moral emotions can alert us that something is going on that requires our attention and consideration; for example, an experience of indignation at someone being abused in our work context focuses our attention on the abusive action and situation, and motivates us to consider how we might intervene. Second, moral emotions provide a basis for association that rapidly connects an experience or object with positive or negative emotions, in such a way that it leads to a more or less automatic response, without thoughtful engagement. A good example would be shame for being caught in some minor social transgression – you don't analyze the situation on the basis of the shame, you just stop the behavior. Third, moral emotions form a self-regulation system that helps individuals adjust, including how they express emotions, in response to experienced or anticipated feedback from others. Think, for example, of the kinds of ways you might express yourself with a trusted friend as opposed to some authority figure. This regulation helps us to "fit in" within a particular social context. Fourth, moral emotions form a key part of a social communication system that signals, often in embodied ways, our internal states to others to facilitate interaction. For example, think about noticing when someone else is experiencing shame (including blushing) that could be connected with a sense of regret for a transgression against you. That realization may help you both to move on.

The four functions of moral emotions are all helpful in the right situation, but the problem is that they cannot all be executed at the same time because there are key tensions between them, as shown in Figure 3.2. Thus, it will be obvious that rapid associative connection must necessarily occur at the expense of a thoughtful, motivated appraisal of what is going on. This means that there is functional conflict between the effects that moral emotions may have, because sometimes the "wrong" function can be favored (Giner-Sorolla, 2013, 2018). For example, in situations where people feel disempowered, they might experience shame in response to abuse through the rapid association function. This is because the context does not allow

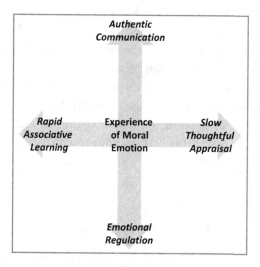

Figure 3.2 Functional conflicts/tensions for moral emotions (opposite functions cannot occur together)

them the freedom to engage in (perfectly justified) anger and appraisal of what is going on if they have been shamed by someone's discriminatory action. In more complicated circumstances, misdirected functional effects of moral emotions can also lead individuals to inappropriate behaviors that have unhelpful effects on others (Fischer & Manstead, 2016).

Organizations can be home to the full range of moral emotions, but they do not favor all of their possible functions equally and, furthermore, there are usually tacit norms about the different ways that women and men are allowed to express emotions (Gill & Arnold, 2015). Especially in times of crisis, those with management or leadership responsibilities, and those that work with them, are expected to regulate their emotions in order to maintain the effectiveness of the organization (Dasborough, Ashkanasy, Tee & Tse, 2009; Hay, 2014; Lindebaum, 2017; Tee, 2015; Troth et al., 2018). The underlying assumption behind this is that emotions – especially negative emotions – are likely disruptive and that moral emotions are no exception to this rule. For example, Hurt and Welbourne (2008) argued that a collective emotional experience and responsive reaction can grow from the emotional experiences of individuals in a team. Based on this potential for emotional states to spread and converge, they connected certain kinds of dispute with negative moral emotions such as shame, guilt or anger. In contrast, Zembylas (2007) and Lindebaum and Gabriel (2016) have argued how even negative emotions – focusing on moral anger – can support and energize a willingness to take positive action against injustice. Thus, it seems clear that attention to moral emotions, and our options in response to how we experience them, is important.

Overall, attention to emotions can enhance our sense of vulnerability (Brown, 2022), but awareness of our vulnerability also makes us more aware of the potential to learn, grow and change in a particular context (Corlett, Mavin & Beech, 2019). To fully engage with that potential we need to explore emotional reflexive practice, which is discussed in the section that follows.

Emotional reflexive practice

Emotions offer us many kinds of information. One kind is a signal that our current ways of understanding a situation just don't work, that there is no clear way forward and we do not know what to do next. In that kind of context our thoughts can seem inadequate. But the lack of an immediate or easy move to rational understanding, when we have an emotional sensation, is actually an invitation to reflexive practice. This begins with heightened self-reflexivity (Corlett, 2013; Hibbert et al., 2010): a focus on understanding *ourselves* and how we react, rather than trying to understand the situation. However, this can still lead to new possibilities for learning and adaptation – and better ways of understanding and coping with a situation – even if it is a difficult struggle. Hibbert, Beech et al. (2022, p799) note that:

> Despite the potential of the approach, pathways to reflexive learning from emotional experiences are not necessarily straightforward. Emotional reactions to challenging events can result in immediate, un-reflexive surface learning solely focused on recognizing and avoiding similar situations ... Such defensive reactions are understandable; but such emotional "containing" can obstruct the deeper learning through self-reflexive practice that could allow us to be more "at home in ourselves" and respond more effectively in future challenging situations.

Our struggles with reflexive learning and adaptation in response to emotional experiences are complicated by our involvement with others, who may have their own emotional take on a situation and different ways of handling it (Burkitt, 2012). However, the initial basis for emotional reflexive practice is simply to be aware that all of this is going on. The first goal of emotional reflexive practice is therefore to cultivate the necessary awareness, and to recognize the potential for our emotional perceptions to influence how we interact with the world and the people we connect to within it (Hibbert, 2021a). This part of the chapter, therefore, focuses on the reflexive practices that can build on initial perceptions of emotion. If you struggle to pay attention to these perceptions, you may find that going "back to the body" (see the "Embodied reflexive practice" section of Chapter 2) can help you to make space for that. What almost certainly won't work is to try to sidestep your emotions, by a direct jump to reacting to the situation as if there is simply a need for an immediate response. That immediate reaction might just be a sign of a functional conflict (Giner-Sorolla, 2013). In other words: the emotions you experience may be telling you something, in which case you need to listen to the message first before clarifying what the response to it could be.

The emotional perceptions of ourselves and others

One of the first ways to build reflexive practice from emotional perceptions is to consider how others are involved in the experience. That is, it is useful to notice how others in the situation seem to be experiencing emotions and whether we are collectively "regulating" what can be expressed (Niven, Totterdell, Holman & Headley, 2012; Parkinson & Manstead, 2015; Van Kleef, 2014). Think about the dynamics of the situation as a kind of communication pattern, but communication carried on purely on the level of emotions – what my emotions "say" is affected by the "conversation" that is going on, and vice versa. This doesn't mean that we ignore what is *actually* said or done, but we look for the underlying emotional communication too. And this is an area where, at least at first, you want to form an initial impression based on what you are feeling, not what you think. You need to recognize and name the emotion that is being experienced, non-judgmentally, before you begin to ask yourself why you are experiencing it.

The next stage is to bring some reflection to bear, still focusing on the emotions, by shifting the time focus back and forward. Shifting backwards, consider the emotions you brought to the situation and how they affected your action and influenced others. For example, anger tends to maintain its own energy and drive action rather than thought (Lindebaum & Gabriel, 2016), perhaps spurring angry responses in others. In contrast, guilt and shame can lead to dissembling and (self-)deception. Ellemers (2018) explains how experiences of guilt or shame, particularly associated with moral failings, can make people feel so bad about themselves that they try to construct an account that excuses their behavior and diminishes their responsibility, rather than facing up to and admitting a moral failure that feels too hard to bear. Because of the possibility of self-deception, a superficial anger about how a situation has affected us may mask a deeper emotion of guilt or shame that can surface later.

You will also want to reflect on the emotions that others are bringing to the situation. Building on that you can consider whether there is a history of unresolved emotion in the context that could be setting people up in certain ways. It could be the case that even if they were (relatively) emotionally neutral before a situation arises, they were primed to experience certain emotions. Moral emotions in particular can lead to a complex mixture of positive and negative views of oneself and others that extend over time (Boudens, 2005; Fineman, 2006; Körner et al., 2016; Tee, 2015), rendering disputes and difficulties more likely and thereby leading to further troubling experiences of moral emotion. Some of these emotional judgments are particularly enduring, and none more so than corrosive moral emotion of contempt. Once you hold someone (or a group of people) in contempt, you will find ways to justify and maintain this emotion even if this involves contradictions: for example, racists will accuse people from a targeted ethnic group of always being lazy when they see them relaxing, but accuse the same people of always working like animals when they are active and busy (Giner-Sorolla, 2013).

Shifting the perspective forward, you need to consider if there are future-oriented emotions of possibility (Steinbock, 2014) that may be affecting the outcome of a situation. It is worthwhile considering whether the emotions being expressed in the current situation – by you or others – are related to a longer-term emotional outlook of this kind. For example, a long history of shame can lead people into a permanent state of despair, through the experience of stigma. Brown (2022) explains how disadvantaging norms that create experiences of shame for individuals, in a particular context, become internalized. Over longer periods of time, this leads to an experience of stigma, diminished dignity and profound suffering. The longer-term emotional outlook could alternatively be more positive – again, for you and/or others – if hope is brought into the situation. The work of Brown and de Graaf (2013), mentioned earlier, showed how hope could be important even in the context of those suffering from terminal cancer. Other moral emotions can work alongside future-oriented emotions, too. For example, pride in conjunction with hope can influence the future "emotional conversation" and the actions that flow from it (Bernhard & Labaki 2021; Jammaers & Ybema, 2023).

The point of reflections on emotional perceptions, both current and looking backwards and forwards, is to help us understand whether the emotional moment is related to an underlying emotional history or emerging narrative. Metaphorically speaking, we may need to reflect on what the longer-term emotional story is, where that is relevant.

It is also important to reflect on whether the emotions being experienced relate to us as an individual human being or whether they relate to our sense of being part of a group. Moral emotions may be felt more strongly and lead to more pronounced effects when groups that we feel a part of are involved (Dumont, Yzerbyt, Wigboldus & Gordijn, 2003; Fischer & Manstead, 2016). Think about the leader of a country, other than your own, who is particularly disreputable. Now think about the worst leader of your own country in recent times (at the time of writing in the United Kingdom there are, sadly, too many options to choose from). Even if the objective faults of your own leader are less than those of the international comparison, the feelings you experience in relation to your own will likely be deeper and include more disruptive moral emotions, like shame. These feelings can be self-reinforcing, too. Connections to a group level can be associated with a particular moral identity, an idea of who you are that is focused on particular moral characteristics (Aquino & Reed, 2002), that tie us more closely to a group (Rehman Kahn, 2021). These moral identity effects can explain how collectively experienced moral emotions can lead to particularly powerful responses, some of which can be positive. For example, Sharvit, Brambilla, Babush and Colucci (2015) explain how collective guilt (and to a lesser extent collective shame) can help to promote behaviors that seek to reverse the harm, or provide compensation, to those who have been affected by a collective moral failure. Thus, the significant and amplifying effects of connection to a collective mean that it is important to understand whether an experience or observation of moral emotion, in a particular situation, has some group-level underpinning. This is a relevant consideration even if only one member of a group is present in the context: we all feel connected to the groups that are important for our self-understanding, even if they are not present with us at the time.[2]

Considering functional conflicts in emotional reflexive practice

If the situation still proves to be difficult to understand – it's hard to follow how the emotional patterns are working out the way that they are – some reflection on potential functional conflicts (Giner-Sorolla, 2013, 2018) may help. This is because the emotional history of the context and the existence of influential group connections may create a strong and specific regulatory climate for emotions. A strong regulatory climate can skew how we use the functions of moral emotions, and three possibilities are worth considering: association instead of appraisal; obvious inauthenticity and undermined relationships; and regulatory suppression of appraisal. In situations when the emotional story does not seem to make sense, it is worth considering whether any of these effects may help us to understand what is going on.

Association instead of appraisal

The effects and pathways associated with the experience of moral emotions in organizations can be complex, and can lead to counterintuitive effects that move problems from one person to another or expand them rather than resolve them (Troth, Townsend, Loudon & Burgess, 2023). An example is offered by Warren et al. (2022), who describe how, when an ally confronts sexism in the workplace, the expression of moral anger is significant (underlining the earlier argument of Lindebaum & Gabriel (2016) about the potential positive effects of expressing anger). They show that the actions of an organizational leader who was an ally were seen in a more favorable light if they were angry while confronting prejudice. Favorable impressions were generated for the organization as well as the leader-ally in cases where anger was expressed, although it also led to polarization within the organization: while some were more likely to support the victim, others were more likely to engage in victim blaming. Warren et al. (2022) concluded that the authentic communication of emotion was an important part of the response, but that the communication should be a moderate, measured expression. In this way, the supportive behavior that is provoked (Fischer & Manstead, 2016; Griessmair, 2017) would be most effective.

A measured expression of anger seems like a difficult balance to achieve. In addition, what is felt to be "measured and appropriate" by one person might be received in different ways by a range of others, pointing to a need for thoughtful engagement with moral emotion on both sides (and reflection on these patterns, as mentioned earlier). This also has a good chance of triggering functional conflict. Moral anger is associated with a motivated appraisal of a situation, a drive to work out what is going on and how to intervene. But the triggered "secondary anger" generated in others in response is not moral but basic, and this is more likely to lead to an instinctual rapid association – it communicates a threat to be resisted, not a call to action. So, if the emotional trajectory is heading off the rails, it may be worth considering whether a functional conflict has been triggered: the situation merited thoughtful appraisal, but a snap-judgment association with a threat (for example) has been the outcome.

Obvious inauthenticity and undermined relationships

Even if a desirable moderation of expression is achieved (Warren et al., 2022), when the regulatory climate stops the authentic communication of emotions other problems can still unfold. For example, Scott, Awasty, Johnson, Matta and Hollenbeck (2020) describe how the transition between a very activated, negative emotional state that is *experienced* to a less active positive emotional state that is *expressed* can seem inauthentic, both for the individual experiencing the emotion and those observing it. This is a significant issue, since moving on from difficult relational problems requires the development of another moral emotion – trust (Steinbock, 2014) – and a sense that someone is not being authentic in how they express themselves will prevent trusting, sustained engagement.

Obvious inauthenticity has another and more particular hazard; it risks evoking the moral emotion of contempt, which tends to be persistent and self-justifying whenever it arises (Giner-Sorolla, 2013; Körner et al., 2016). As I discussed earlier, once an individual feels contempt towards another this perception tends to be stable, to the extent that the individual experiencing contempt of another will vary their descriptions of others to suit the emotion (Giner-Sorolla, 2013). For these reasons, actions or a climate that leads to overregulation of the communication of moral emotions place the proper function of regulation (fitting in with accepted social norms) and authentic communication into conflict. The end result of this is obvious inauthenticity in how we are presenting ourselves. This inauthenticity has potentially negative consequences for the relationship between those experiencing the emotion and those watching this emotional story unfold.

Regulatory suppression of appraisal

Suppression of emotions through overregulation can have a general effect that undermines a careful appraisal of the situation that led to the experience of a moral emotion. The lack of careful appraisal – when it is warranted – undermines the identification of appropriate action in response to the triggering situation (Zembylas, 2007). Thus, Kemp, Cowart and Bui's (2020) study describes how the careful reappraisal of emotions, rather than suppression of their expression, was a more effective strategy for handling troubling emotions. Their study focused on anxiety in particular, but it is possible to speculate that similar insights could be developed in relation to negative moral emotions such as shame, guilt or despair (Giner-Sorolla, 2013; Steinbock, 2014).

In order for a moral emotion handling strategy based on reappraisal to be adopted, expression (the communicative function of moral emotions) will need to be mobilized first. An individual will be limited in effectively reappraising an emotion which has not been experienced *and* expressed, at least to some extent. Our own self-reflexive awareness of emotions begins with fully engaging with the perception, as discussed earlier, and locking down our outward display or expression of the emotion will get in the way of that (Hibbert, Beech et al., 2022). In contrast, expression followed by careful engagement supports an appraisal of an experienced moral emotion, which in turn leads to a better understanding of what is going on in the context in which it arose (Giner-Soralla, 2013, 2018). However, this strategy may be difficult to deploy in overregulated contexts, which sadly includes most organizations (Lindebaum, 2017), where emotional suppression is usually normalized and expected (Troth et al., 2023). In such circumstances, the expression of the moral emotion that would bring it to the foreground of our awareness may not take place. Thus, particularly in organizational contexts and other overregulated emotional climates, the meaningful (re)appraisal that can be a useful response to moral emotions can be suppressed.

The importance of exploring functional conflicts

Conflicts between the functions of moral emotions, and the emotional stories leading to the "wrong" function in a given situation, are problematic for people in organizations. This is because there is a qualitative, significant difference between basic emotions like fear and more complex moral emotions. Parker (2022), focusing on a general sense of unease or unrest associated with a complex emotional experience, explains that a sense of unrest is a message to pay attention, but this message is sent through "survival circuitry" that is also used to trigger fight-or-flight responses. With the potential for unhelpful reactions to be triggered, arguments about limiting the contagion of basic emotions at times of crisis seem sound enough (Tee, 2015; Troth et al., 2018). But against that, the experience of *moral* emotions – when they are not channeled into inappropriately *basic* responses – can be a motivation for important action. For example, when the appropriate response is not diverted by functional conflict, moral emotions can support action against inappropriate conduct by the members or leaders of an organization (Warren et al., 2022; Wijaya & Heugens, 2018). More generally, moral emotions can motivate a careful appraisal of the context in which something is felt to be unjust, inappropriate or plain wrong (Lindebaum & Gabriel, 2016). These are all positive effects that organizations would wish to promote, and leaders should want people to tell them when they are taking inappropriate actions. However, because of the functional conflicts that can happen, often through excessive regulation, enabling the positive potential of moral emotions may be difficult to achieve. For that reason, it can be worth trying to work out if one of the three potential functional conflicts explored above could be involved in how a situation is unfolding, especially in the context of your leader work.

Emotional reflexive practice and leader work

Developing reflexive practice to include attention to emotions can contribute to the development of our leader work. There are two main areas to focus on in relation to that. The first is to consider how we engage with the reflexive practices outlined above, in situations of leadership when emotions are running ahead of our thoughts. The second is to reflect on the way in which we might seek to influence organizations to have more space for attention to emotions, so that others may also have the opportunity to engage in careful emotion work (Hochschild, 1979) and reflexive practice.

Crafting space for emotional reflexive practice

Emotional reflexive practice involves honoring the emotional perceptions that we have but also involves going beyond that. The four steps outlined earlier move from the immediate perceptions of our own and others' emotions, through reflection on the emotional history and then the trajectory of the situation, to (if necessary) exploring possible functional conflict mechanisms for why the evolving emotional story might be counterintuitive. But that kind of engagement with emotions feels like a lot to handle in the busyness of everyday organizational life, let alone when we are in the middle of a crisis or a situation that feels traumatic (Greenberg &

Hibbert, 2020). We may need to be careful about when we engage in that depth of practice and explore two alternative ways of handling it.

One way to provide the space for engaging with and reflecting on emotions is to make time for them as they emerge in a given situation. This may seem counterintuitive (or even impossible) given the normal pace of organizational life, but we need to question why we sometimes behave like emergency department doctors in our everyday work environments.[3] Because suppressing emotions can interfere with our analysis and learning in a situation (Giner-Sorolla, 2013, 2018) we need to be careful only to be in "crisis mode" when there truly is a crisis. Otherwise, ramp up the stress and eventually, for *everyone*, instant decisions will be based on limited information and will likely involve emotional functional conflicts – and therefore lead to mistakes. Instead, be ready to slow things down, refuse to make snap judgments and allow everyone time to process what is going on (Hibbert, 2015). In contrast, if there really is a crisis – the building is literally or metaphorically on fire – you will know the difference. No one debates what to do when they face real danger, there are more basic mechanisms that take over.

However, if you are really under pressure in a situation, there is another alternative for emotional reflexive practice. That is to provide space later, perhaps through working with others, to reflect on the situation. It's likely that an intense emotional experience will heighten your memory of a situation anyway (Hibbert, Beech et al., 2022), which helps to make this possible. But you will need to be careful of carrying your own emotional pain for too long – if that is part of the experience – and be sure not to try to analyze a situation if your own pain is serious and unresolved. You will not be able to get enough critical distance if that is the case, and getting help with your own injury should come first and will require time. A process for engaging with deferred emotion, with the help of trusted colleagues, is suggested by Hibbert, Beech et al. (2022, p811):

> [With] legitimation for acknowledging rather than regretting our emotional responses, deeper and more authentically expressive emotion work was enabled ... Acknowledging emotions in this way may entail more statements about what people experience themselves and less about what they believe others are "making" them feel. [We found that when] we had fully established a supportive context with open and trusting relationships, [this] enabled us to reanalyze and reinterpret

stories in this way. Helpful attention of others was therefore found to be useful in developing learning from emotional experiences ... Our open and trusting relationships – and the compassionate aware-ness of each other's concerns – enabled us, in time, to move beyond the emotional difficulty of the stories (Ramsey, 2008) and to develop learning insights that could be useful for the "owner" of the story and others (Beets & Goodman 2012; Hibbert et al., 2019) faced with simi-lar organizational situations.

The point of all of this careful reflexive practice is, most of the time, to work on the only emotional system that is even marginally under your direct control – your own. That doesn't mean that you can choose your emotions any more than anyone else, but you can be more aware of what they mean and how they are involved in your communication with others. I recognize, though, that not every instance of emotion you see is going to need to be unpacked and engaged with through focused reflexive practice. Maybe someone in the organization got a parking fine, or got engaged, or has been bereaved or ... you get the picture. We all bring our emotions into situations from our daily lives, and these are not necessarily part of the emotional narrative of the organization. In these cases, just noticing the emotion and showing genuine human interest (or compassion) may be all that is needed. And that is leader work, too.

Changing how organizations accommodate emotions

Allowing more space for emotions cannot mean that "anything goes", and we may still face crisis situations where we have to hold things together while dealing with an emergency. So, we need to think about whether there are more positive forms of emotion regulation that can provide space for expres-sion, without a risk of losing control. These better forms of regulation may apply to particular situations, rather than the whole range of organizational life. For example, Alam and Singh (2021) highlight how emotional regu-lation can be helpful during performance feedback. They advocate a kind of holding space, crafted through dialogue, so that feelings can be worked through, even when this might involve difficult moral emotions like shame or guilt. The "holding space" of dialogue explored in their work connects with insights about the role of trust in moving on from encounters that lead to negative moral emotions (Hibbert, Mavin et al., 2022; Steinbock, 2014).

EMOTIONS AND LEADER WORK   59

Alam and Singh's (2021) work calls into question whether the dominant, negative view of emotion regulation in organizations is the only side of the coin. It is still the case that the emotion work that regulation places on individuals may be associated with inauthenticity (Hochschild, 1979) and thereby potentially contribute to stress and burnout (Ashkanasy, Humphrey & Huy, 2017). But if there is a more developed and deliberate supportive process to hold and explore the functions of moral emotions, namely reflexive dialogue (Hibbert, Beech et al., 2022), more positive outcomes are possible. This is because a process of dialogue allows for a balance of expression and constructive critique, which leads to ideas and insights for adaptation. I discuss dialogue in much more detail in Chapter 5, where I explore relationships and relational reflexivity in depth, but there are some general points that we can focus on here. I suggest that three connected lines of action, enabling emotional reflexivity, can be useful for organizations. Leader work can include helping these actions to be achieved.

First, organizations should develop a climate in which self-reflexivity is supported, thereby enabling members to have better awareness of (and about) their experiences of moral emotions (Hibbert, 2021a; Hibbert, Beech et al., 2022).

Second, interpersonal processes – especially where they relate to performance, development or conduct issues – should be built around relationally reflexive processes of dialogue (Hibbert, Mavin et al., 2022) that provide a supportive context for emotional communication along with an expectation of learning and adaptation, building on and adapting the insights of Alam and Singh (2021) and Lindebaum and Gabriel (2016). In short, organizations need to become contexts in which the expression of moral emotions is seen to be an intrinsic part of communication processes – but not the only part.

The third action is to accept the vulnerability that this kind of organizational climate will create for leaders. Here we do not mean the kind of structural vulnerability that simply places someone at risk with no upside (Brown, 2022), but instead the elective vulnerability (Corlett et al., 2019) that allows for leaders to be open to learning and changing. Hibbert, Mavin et al. (2022, p20) summed up their research in this area in this way:

the trajectories we explored show that the vulnerability experienced through "toxic handling" (Frost & Robinson, 1999) or traumatic situations (Hibbert et al, 2022) can be important learning points that change how leaders develop and ... how "... individuals' willingness to take positive action in difficult circumstances" (Hibbert et al., 2019:189) avoids amoral pragmatism or equanimity. This is important since there are situations, in which leadership is enacted, that should feel dangerous and even hurt [us], if we are to remain connected to our moral anchors. Embracing vulnerability, learning from and in vulnerability, in the context of dialogic reflexive learning with highly trusted others, can be a means of adaptation and challenge to heroic identities and mechanistic conceptualizations of organization. Such dialogic emotional engagement highlights how vulnerability in leadership is sometimes unresolved, as well as offering new perspectives on future action.

The end results of taking on emotional reflexive practice in leader work could be transformational for leaders and organizations. The transformative potential does not arise purely through the reflexive practices themselves, but through the development of an enhanced emotional repertoire. A developed repertoire of emotional engagement in the processes of leader work might include:

> options beyond control and containment in contexts where, for example, the expression of anger or grief might be recognized as legitimate (Saam, 2018). [Through reflexive practice] the process will enhance both their repertoires and their ability to connect with emotional experience ... We believe that enhancing repertoires of emotion work leads to an enhanced ability to be able to deal with situations that give rise to powerful negative emotions, while also avoiding a traumatic burden associated with long-term emotional containment.
>
> (Hibbert, Beech et al., 2022, p813)

Summary and actions

In this chapter I have explored the role of emotions in general, and moral emotions in particular, in shaping and informing our experiences. Emotions can affect us immediately, in a particular situation, or affect us later through (triggered) memories. In either case they alert us to some potential information about a situation (and ourselves) that is worth noting, taking care as we do so to avoid the traps that firing up the wrong response can lead to. I have also shown how engaging with emotional experiences, through four reflexive practice steps, can help us to better understand the emotions of ourselves and others. We do so by "staying with" the emotional story before trying to shift into thoughtful analysis. If you are looking for ways to begin applying these insights in your leader work, you will find suggestions below.

Evaluate your readiness to engage with emotions

Engaging with emotions may not be easy and you should seek professional help if you feel that you need it. Alternatively, if you feel that you are just dealing with everyday stress that makes it hard to find the necessary focus to get started, you might benefit from reviewing the embodied reflexive practice suggestions set out earlier in this chapter, that apply the insights from Chapter 2. The practice of centering (or other similar mindfulness or yoga techniques that work for you, if they are part of your practice) may be a good place to start.

Develop the four steps of emotional reflexive practice

As a reminder, the steps of emotional reflexive practice begin with attention to our immediate perceptions of our own and others' emotions, move through reflection on the emotional history and then the trajectory of the situation, and may proceed to exploring possible functional conflict mechanisms if the evolving emotional story seems to be counterintuitive. Where it is possible, you should seek to engage with these reflexive practices when an emotionally intense situation arises. But you could also engage in unpacking the situation with trusted friends or colleagues at a later time (as discussed in Chapter 5, there are reasons why that might be a good idea anyway).

Consider building a small reflexive practice group

As mentioned earlier, working through emotional experiences at a later time is more productive when you can explore the situation with trusted friends or colleagues. It is going to be most useful to you and them if this small group (say, three or four people): understand your work or professional context but are not in the same organization; have reciprocal relationships of trust and confidentiality, built on mutual sharing and vulnerability; and are close enough for honesty, but not so close that they would struggle to tell you when you might have done something wrong.

Consider how you might change the organizational climate

If you have the opportunity to do leader work in the organization, think about how that might use your established or emergent position to build a more favorable regulatory climate in relation to the expression of emotions. The goal is to allow everyone to benefit from the information that emotions can bring to us, and live authentic emotional lives, without that being the whole story. To help achieve that balance, the insights in Chapter 4 on thought and in Chapter 5 on relationships should prove to be useful.

Notes

1 Identity work is discussed in detail in Chapter 6.
2 For more on this theme, see Chapter 6.
3 Unless, of course, you *are* an emergency department doctor – in which case, please continue!

4

THOUGHT AND LEADER WORK

Noticing our thinking

We all make mistakes and have some regrets. That is inevitable. But we need to be able to distinguish between the effects of chance, that we have to accept, from opportunities to change our approach in the future. Reflexive thought begins with looking back – sometimes with a feeling of shock – at how we have acted and the choices we made that were clearly wrong. We might also notice how our choices were built on dubious assumptions that we took for granted. Or, because we are socialized into a particular way of thinking and acting in our communities and organizations, sometimes we are not even aware of possible questions we should ask about what is going on (Hibbert & Huxham, 2010; Shils, 1981). It can also surprise others when our questions and concerns are different from their expectations.

A PERSONAL STORY: INTUITIVE WISDOM – OR NOT?

The union at our organization was heading for a vote on strike action. The senior management team, in one of our regular meetings, was trying

---

DOI: 10.4324/9781032721507-4

to decide what we should say about the issues behind the strike vote in a public statement. It was a strained discussion and eventually we hammered out an agreed text that would be released after the vote had concluded. It was a good and fair message that showed the points where we were all on the same side. The chair was relieved that the meeting item seemed to be over and asked if we were all content. I said "no". It was a difficult moment! But I explained how the text was fine, but I felt the situation was finely balanced and that we should release the public message *before* the union voted on strike action. That was accepted, and the message was released earlier than originally intended. The union failed to win support for the strike action, falling short by just two votes.

Afterwards, a colleague praised me for my intuition about the vote outcome. I had to be honest: I confessed that I had no idea whether the message would have an effect on the vote or not – I was more concerned about how the senior management team would feel, and what the staff would think, if we had not even tried to make a difference and the vote had gone the other way.

I have shared the story above not to suggest that my intervention made any difference – I have no way of knowing that – but to underline how we could all be thinking different things in a discussion that are not obvious to others, and relying on intuition and imagination as well as logic. I intuited the vote would be close, but was guided by my imagination about how people might feel afterwards, whatever happened. It was a moral and emotional point for me, as much as a practical concern.

When new experiences help us to see that our ways of thinking should not remain unchallenged, the questions that confront us often have both moral and practical importance. So, in this chapter, I focus on thought and its connection to leader work in three main sections. The first section considers thought, its connection to our past and future and its limitations. The second section sets out how we can develop our critical awareness through thoughtful reflexive practice. The third section explains how thoughtful reflexive practice can inform leader work. These three main sections are followed by a brief summary and suggested actions for implementation.

Thinking about the past, present and future

The link between the past and reflexive thought is fundamental. Our capacity for thinking and judging is necessarily built on our past experience – where else could it come from? Thus, our ways of thinking will be influenced by formal learning but also by much more than that, as we learn to interpret what is going on. Davey (2006) argues that if we have long experience of thoughtfully interpreting our situations and possibilities, we will be less likely to fall into the trap of making hasty judgments or relying on initial impressions and more likely to make wise choices. However, he also points out that there is no single program or method that provides a short cut to this kind of wisdom. It takes experience, awareness and time.

Knowing that our thinking is built on our past experience, reflexivity helps us to see what aspects of our history we are building on when we think in a particular way. To put it another way, reflexive thought is a process of thinking about our thinking (Myers, 2010), but this is complicated given the fact that we have to use our experience as the basis of interpretation. We can feel that we are caught in a loop (Hibbert et al., 2010). Nevertheless, we can still try to describe where we are standing in order to describe our viewpoint, even if we know we can never quite dig down to the bedrock beneath our feet, because it is interpretation all the way down (Davey, 2006; Gadamer, 1998; Hibbert et al., 2017).

A critical lens on the past

Even if we can never dig down to a fundamental truth in understanding our viewpoint and how we came to it, self-examination is still important. Unless we bring some challenge to our engagement with experience, then we are just "automatically adapting" to it rather than exploring different ways to respond and grow (Hibbert et al., 2010). That could mean either that you never step beyond the bounds of the traditions that you grew up in, or conversely that you let yourself be so easily influenced that you are changed in ways that can lead you to forget who you are (or want to be: Cunliffe, 2018). To tackle this, we need to add to self-reflexivity by also looking at our experience through the lens of critical reflexivity. Adopting a critically reflexive attitude leads us to ask why we interpret our experiences – and the world – in the ways that we do.

The answer to the critically reflexive question is simple, in some ways. We all come from somewhere, and have lived and grown in distinctive family groups or other distinctive early life contexts. We learned to navigate life in countries with particular political systems, were nurtured or challenged by particular cultures and/or religions and learned to talk and think in particular languages. All of these influences lead us to interpret, understand and act on the world in particular ways (Aronowitz, Deener, Keene, Schnittker & Tach, 2015; Hibbert et al., 2017; Hibbert et al., 2010; Hibbert & Huxham, 2010, 2011). The effect of all of the cultural, social and ideological influences on our thought does not mean that people turn out to be "cookie-cutter" types in a particular context. We should remember that we have bodies and emotions and we experience the world in unique ways through those, too. Our backgrounds interact with the embodied and emotional aspects of ourselves to lead to a variety of different experiences for people, even if they are in the same place at the same time. For example, if you have sisters or brothers, think about how different you were, even when growing up in the same household. In addition, most modern societies tend to be diverse and are woven from a variety of different cultures. There may be multiple influences on our lives and development in a given context, although we need to be alert to the fact that some people may not have the same privileged access to cultural and contextual resources that we might have (Namatende-Sakwa, 2018).

In any case, we are all strongly shaped by the traditions of our particular communities (Hibbert & Huxham, 2010, 2011; Shils, 1981) and they provide us with the language and concepts we think with. So, no-one can stand entirely apart from their history, education and formation as a totally neutral or objective observer (Cunliffe, 2003; Hibbert et al., 2010). But we can turn the concepts that have shaped us against themselves. Any concept implies its opposite, and that becomes available to us too (Gadamer, 1998). You can look at how common binary opposite conflicts are in politics and the relationships between nations for evidence of this. That means that we don't necessarily take on board every experience without questioning (Archer, 2007), but it also underlines the importance of traditions and their opposites in framing alternatives, which can still leave something taken for granted. Think, for example, about how Philip Pullman's masterpiece *His Dark Materials* trilogy uses some traditional religious ideas and imagery to nevertheless develop an atheistic story (which aligns with his own perspective), and how the narrative opens in a very traditional academic setting. Even if we resist the traditions and cultural understandings that shaped us, we might still have a hand in perpetuating them and making them meaningful for others.

Overall, the lens of critical reflexivity helps us to see how our past experiences have shaped us and influenced how we interpret new experiences. In earlier work (Hibbert, 2021a), I explained the three key realizations that flow from this, and how those insights invite certain forms of action in response. In the points below I build on these insights to give a stronger focus on the action potential they provide:

Revealing our background: We need to decide if and how we deliberately acknowledge our formation, based on the knowledge that the interpretations that we make are influenced by the traditions and ideologies that shaped our personal development (Hibbert et al., 2017; Shils, 1981). This is something that we rarely do, even for ourselves. What is the story of how your upbringing shaped you, and what do you learn when you try to tell this story?

Recognizing (dis)advantage: We need to consider the alternative choices we have about how to act when we recognize that our formative cultural traditions may carry norms that privilege some and exclude or diminish others (Namatende-Sakwa, 2018). What doors are open for you, and what doors are closed against you?

Resisting passive transmission: If we interpret uncritically and act unthinkingly, we perpetuate without question the traditional positions and ideologies which were influential in our formation. We need to decide whether and how we should interrupt our role in this process of transmission to allow more room for the understandings of others (Hibbert et al., 2014). What assumptions are you tacitly sharing in what you do and say?

Recognizing how we have been shaped and influenced, and that we influence others in similar ways, does not mean that we can simply set all of that aside and deploy some kind of "Vulcan logic".[1] We cannot entirely jump beyond the ideas and influences that have shaped us because we think with the language and tools they have provided. However, we can continue to struggle with the challenge of questioning our assumptions, reflect on our choices about how to live and who to be, and so try to generate possibilities that go beyond our initial understandings (Cunliffe, 2004).

Turning the lens on ourselves and our futures

Cunliffe's (2004) perspective on challenging our assumptions moves us from looking back at the past that shaped us to thinking about how we might act in the future. That also entails a return from critical reflexivity back to self-reflexivity, to consider how we adapt to everyday experience using the internal resources that are available to us. As we have seen (in Chapters 2 and 3), this includes forms of bodily awareness and emotional perceptions, but it also involves thought.

We might recognize the idea of self-reflexivity from our "internal conversation" when we mull over what is going on in and around us. Margaret Archer sees this as an inescapable and inalienable human activity (Archer, 2007). However, while the idea of an internal conversation is a reasonable and recognizable concept, it does not capture everything that is going on. Our self-reflexive adaptation certainly builds on our life experiences and is always happening (Caetano, 2017; Hibbert et al., 2010; Hibbert et al., 2017). But this adaptation does not always involve noticeable internal work, whether that might be through an internal conversation or some other process. Instead, it can also include external conversations and interactions with others that might not be planned, and/or a mixture of internal and external processes (Gilmore & Kenny, 2015; Hibbert, Beech et al., 2022).

Clearly there is still some thought going on when we interact with others, and it must build on our past experience. However, we do not usually stop and think about what to say during a conversation. Most of the time, conversation just flows: our decisions about what to say next (or what to do next) are not usually worked out through a painstaking process of consciously weighing up all the available information. Instead, for much of the time we mobilize – in a much more unconscious way – rules of thumb or heuristics. These provide the basis for our intuitive engagement with the world. Gigerenzer (2008) has called intuition the "steering wheel" for life and argued – based on persuasive evidence – that human intelligence need not always involve conscious thought. He explains how there are lots of everyday rules that we know how to apply (like grammar) without all being able to explain what the rules are. This is the domain of tacit knowing (Polanyi, 1966: in short, we know more than we can say). Gigerenzer (2008) sets out a wide range of situations in which such intuitive thinking is effective. To be reflexive, we may need to become more aware of using such intuitive heuristics. However, heuristics might still be the best approach to a task under certain conditions, especially when our experience and skills have been developed to support a particular sort of practice. Indeed, "stop thinking when you are skilled" is one of the heuristics illustrated by Gigerenzer (2008). To illustrate this, he recounts the example of a famous musician who could only overcome a mental block, while rehearsing a very familiar passage of music, by turning on every source of noise in his house. With so much noise the musician was literally unable to think, and was again able to play through the particular piece of music without seizing up at the blocked passage. Thinking about it was getting in the way of his embodied skill.

As well as heuristics, there is another kind of thought (or component of it) that stretches our patterns of thinking further: that is, imagination. If you have ever had a weird dream you will know how far imagination can stretch. But it doesn't have to go all the way to fantasy to add to "rational" thought in useful ways. I would like to highlight three things that imagination brings to our thoughts.

First, imagination *fills in the gaps* enough for us to understand something well enough, without all the details. We bring together ideas from our memories with information from our senses (Thompson, 2018) in order to *contextualize* our current experience (Hibbert, 2021a). If you consider your experience of reading a novel, you will recognize that writers usually give you only a "sketch" of each character's appearance or how a particular scene looks. You might not be able to draw the people or the place if asked, but the text gives you enough to go on to connect it all up into a reasonable story (assuming that the novel *has* a reasonable story!).

Second, imagination allows us to *explore alternative models or frames.* Although our background and culture provide the lenses through which we see the world (Hibbert et al., 2017), we can still ask "what if …?" and see how the world looks through other lenses (Gabriel, 2018; Pless, Sengupta, Wheeler & Maak, 2022). Tienari (2022) sees this aspect of imagination as both a personal and a social capacity, informed by our actual or "armchair" travel in different communities. Such experiences show us different ways of understanding the world. This means that the contextualization of our experience is not limited by reference to "reality", but can be taken into new territories through imagination, which can draw on art and literature just as easily and beneficially as it might draw on facts and formal theories (Hibbert et al., 2017). Examples of how far this can take us include the fact that geostationary communications satellites were proposed in 1945 by the science fiction writer Arthur C. Clarke, and numerous later inventions were first imagined in the science fiction series *Star Trek*. People miss a great deal when they reject imaginative fiction, but I hope they live long and prosper, nonetheless.

Third, imagination allows us to *improvise*. The point of understanding our experience is to be able to *conceptualize* it (Hibbert, 2021a), to be able to say something about it, even if only to ourselves in our internal conversation. Then, based on that conceptualization, we can shape thoughtful options for taking action. Through imagination's help in "filling in the gaps" and the way it provides alternative ways of seeing the world, our thoughts can generate a wider range of possible actions. For this reason, complex moral challenges often require imagination (Pless et al., 2022), as do the challenges that are experienced in moments of leadership, when there is the need to find some possibility for action even in seemingly impossible circumstances (Judson, 2020). Through imagination our conceptualizations, in challenging situations, can include alternatives that take us beyond our default, familiar responses. At such times imagination and intuition overlap, and it can be difficult to unpack and explain precisely how innovative ideas were generated.

So, if self-reflexivity is a process of "thinking about how we think" in order to change it (Hibbert et al., 2010), we need to be aware that some of that thinking might be harder to identify and isolate than we imagined, and it could be disruptive to try. Neither intuition (Gigerenzer, 2008) or imagination (Judson, 2020; Thompson, 2018; Tienari, 2022) are easily unpacked through introspection. Nevertheless, self-reflexivity can lead to more thoughtfulness, by helping to support three kinds of change (derived from Hibbert, 2021a):

Changed thinking: if we develop a new and different understanding of some person, object or system in our social context, we will be able to think differently about the situations and events in which they are involved.

Changed relationships: New and different understandings of people, situations and events are likely to lead to new and different ways of interacting with the people we meet in those contexts.

Changed selves: With revised understandings of people, situations and events, and reconfigured relationships, we can make new and different choices about how we can best survive, thrive and develop in a given context.

Despite the focus on change and the future orientation of self-reflexivity, the conundrum is that – given our intuitive actions and the flow of activities like conversation – deliberate reflexive practice is going to require some examination of the very recent past. Ultimately, then, self-reflexivity goes hand in hand with critical reflexivity (Hibbert, 2021a) and also benefits from our engagement with others who provide a different lens on our experience (Ripamonti, Galuppo, Gorli, Scaratti & Cunliffe, 2017). I will focus on the importance of relationships in Chapter 5, but for the moment we need to focus on how we can engage with and reinterpret our experience as close to the moment of action as possible, through constructing thoughtful reflexive practice.

Thoughtful reflexive practice

If thoughtful reflexive practice is to take account of our past and help us to be more aware of our future possibilities for change, then it needs to involve processes that help us look in both directions. Here I will explore two options for examining the past, and two for entertaining different future possibilities.

Reflexive questioning of the past

Using a different lens

If we begin with the past, one way of unearthing taken-for-granted assumptions is to try to deliberately pick up a different "lens" to examine our experience (Hibbert, 2013; Hibbert and Cunliffe, 2015). It's helpful to pick something that seems different or unfamiliar from your usual "comfort zone". For example, if you can handle it, what happens when you examine a situation from the point of view of a competitor, or someone with opposite political views from your own, or someone with a different faith or philosophy of life? To do this usefully, you have to ask yourself the question "what if they are right?" and see what conclusions follow. Sometimes you will find it an uncomfortable experience.

The point of entertaining such different viewpoints is not to change your mind in order to accept them wholesale, but instead to see what shows up and how it might challenge some of your assumptions. For example, Hibbert and Cunliffe (2015) report how an executive MBA student, who was based in a large company in the Middle East, described how his views were changed after exploring a feminist viewpoint. He recognized the limited opportunities for women in his company and broader society, and committed to advocacy and providing the maximum opportunities for education and self-expression for his daughters.

Deconstruction

Entertaining different viewpoints helps us to be suspicious of the assumptions that are seen as normal in our contexts. A second and more radical way to look for the influences that shape our interpretation of experiences, and to help us to be suspicious about them, is to use techniques from deconstruction (Derrida, 1976, 1978). Deconstruction exposes some unavoidable facts that go along with a particular view of the world: one way of looking at things is always at the expense of other viewpoints; if something is in the foreground it probably hides something in the background; and when a specific person(s) is speaking or writing, others are not able to do so. In organization studies, deconstruction is typically used to expose the interests that someone has "hidden" in their choice of words, usually in writing (although it can also apply to speech). While it can seem that this is critically reflexive (because it is, on one level), it is also self-reflexive. That's because if we didn't notice what was being hidden in plain sight, as deconstruction reveals, it is because we have interpreted what we have read (or heard) as normal. In such cases, we have been socialized into, and accepted without question, the assumptions on which some text or speech is constructed.

Undertaking deconstruction is theoretically complex but does not have to be difficult in practice. A set of questions for using this technique with written texts was assembled by Wright, Middleton, Hibbert and Brazil (2020), who used their approach with people from a wide variety of organizations and professions. In the points that follow, I have adapted the description and application of their questions to suit the purpose of this book, and added illustrative examples. I am sorry that the examples are largely political, but politics provides so much in the way of biased communication that it is something of an easy target!

What is the storyline? This allows us to – perhaps with the benefit of imagination – see what the underlying story behind some writing or talk is. Think, for example, about the implied story behind a political slogan like "Get Brexit Done". There is an implicit characterization of a problem and some implied desirable future in the background, even if these are never explored and/or may even be quite misleading.

Are there dichotomies? Asking this question allows us to see if opposite points of view are being suppressed in writing or talk. Think about how changes to employment contracts in industrial disputes are always described as "modernization". Modern means it must be new and better, right? But if you look at the suppressed point of view you will see the changes usually include less flexible working conditions and fewer benefits – and so they are not better for everyone and are actually a return to older and less enlightened employment practices in many ways.

Are there silences? If we ask this question then we can see what remains unsaid in writing or talk, and/or who does not get the chance to be heard. A good example (at the time of writing) is the treatment of refugees in politics in the United Kingdom. In hours of national television news and debate, I cannot recall one single interview with a refugee.

What are the contradictions? This question helps us to see if what is being said is based on conflicting ideas or is perverting one principle in favor of another that is dominant. For example, imagine describing a *peace* plan that does not undo the damage and losses experienced by an invaded nation: that would show that *aggression* is rewarded.

Can the story be resituated? Having challenged the underlying story on many levels, you can then see what else might be going on. In all of the examples I have given for the first four questions, you would be able to determine that there are particular people who are being oppressed, while others are being advantaged. That may be the objective, from the implicit perspective of the person who is able to control what is said or written.

If you see any of the illustrative examples above as unproblematic that does not mean that you are right or wrong – but it does mean that you have decided that the relevant underlying assumption that is revealed is valid from your perspective. Still, you should at least be able to see that others might legitimately take a different view, and so look at similar points in the future with greater flexibility.

Reflexive exploration of the future

Reflexive thought about our past involves using different perspectives and asking critical questions, and the same approach feeds into how we understand future possibilities. My focus here, though, is on the possibilities that open up at a particular time rather than mapping out the future in detail (as if that was possible). Nevertheless, a reflexive take on the past does help us to mobilize our experience so that we can develop future actions (Maclean, Harvey & Chia, 2012) and can also help us tie these plans into motivating emotional trajectories, especially those involving hope (Hibbert, Beech et al., 2022; Hibbert, Mavin et al., 2022). While this is a more or less analytical approach, there are two particular ways of mobilizing thoughtful reflexive practice that can add to it, through using intuition and imagination.

Using intuition

I have already introduced the idea of intuition, and I follow Gigerenzer (2008) in my conviction that our innate capacities and heuristics (rules of thumb) quickly inform our interpretation of what is going on moment by moment and can often guide appropriate action. The trick for reflexive practice, of course, is to know when trusting intuition might be the best option. Gigerenzer (2008) suggests four conditions, which I describe here as:

Highly unpredictable systems: In cases of highly volatile and unpredictable systems – for example, stock markets – intuitive judgment may work as well or better than the analyses of experts who rely on knowledge that is always insufficient for prediction.

Tasks requiring physical skills: Intuitive judgments based on embodied skills are debased by attempts to think through the details (much like the case of the musician with a mental block).

The risk of information overload: Too much information would prevent us from being able to make decisions and choosing how to act, and the way our brains work (including forgetting things!) helps to prevent this potential for overload. So, when the information is overwhelming, heuristics may be the best option.

The risk of option overload: In a similar way to the problem of information overload, having too many options about how to act may cause confusion (or conflict, if several people are involved in making a choice). So, it may be easier to rely on a simple rule of thumb in such cases.

I can also summarize those insights in a simpler form: if you are uncertain and either don't have enough information or there is too much to assimilate, and/or you have a lot of experience of making judgments in the area, ask yourself what your "gut instinct" is. What is your hunch about what is going on, and what should you do in response? Reflexivity can work hand in hand with intuition (Elbanna, 2015), but I suggest that most of the time you need to challenge your intuition with some simple reflexive questioning before you accept it. I offer these considerations:

Check your body and emotions: are you tired, in pain, angry, sad ... how might your current bodily and emotional state be impacting on your judgment and intuition? This is part of the reason that we looked at those levels first (see Chapters 2 and 3). Remember that your body and emotions are also sources of information, and not just distractions.

Check the context: how we think – including intuitive thought – is influenced by the situation and what is going on around us. For example, you should definitely trust your gut instinct *less* in the face of sales techniques. Is your judgment being manipulated?

Check the consequences: unless there is so little time that you have no choice, weigh up the likely downsides if your interpretation is wrong. This is not much use to you by itself, but may lead you to consider the next point.

Check for others with more experience or expertise: do you have to trust your intuition, or might someone else you can connect with have a more informed view that can be mobilized in a useful way? The key here is to identify someone with robust information that you can trust (I explore how to work with others' insights in more detail in Chapter 5). For example, you might have intuitive ways to decide what to plant in your garden (having unconsciously recognized common plants grown in your neighborhood) and that may work well enough. But a professional gardener might quickly spot differences in your soil, evidence of pests, the position of your garden in relation to sun and wind and so on.

What follows from these checks may still be a decision to go with your intuitive interpretation – either because of a lack of time, no evident serious consequences or a lack of alternative ways to reach an understanding of the situation. But at least you will be *aware* that you are relying on intuition and heuristics, and you can be more comfortable about doing so. It may still be the best option.

Develop your capacity for imagination

Another way of challenging your interpretations, and the future action choices that follow them, is the option to use your imagination. In some ways this connects with past-oriented, critical reflexivity because it draws your attention to the world on a larger scale. The point is to think about larger structures and influences – such as culture and society – but to do so with a view to understanding how you are maintaining or building them (Hibbert et al., 2010) and the responsibilities that follow from that realization (Hibbert & Cunliffe, 2015). The central skill here is to nurture and use three kinds of imagination.

Creative imagination (Pless et al., 2022; Saggurthi & Thakur 2016): Almost all of us have the capacity for imagination on some level. Think about the little child making up a fantasy world in their play, or having to write a story in your school days, or think about how you will spend your next vacation. In all of these cases there is no predetermined answer or right way to go. In our day to day lives imagination addresses uncertainty and is a way of developing an understanding of what to do when we cannot know for sure (Saggurthi & Thakur 2016). But you do not work from nothing: the richer your experience the more material your imagination has to work on. It is the *breadth* of experience that counts, not its precise link to the matter in question. So, developing this capacity might be nurtured more effectively through engaging with art and

literature than through everyday experience or professional learning. Artistic encounters can give you alternative frames that help you
understand differently (Hibbert et al., 2017). For example, try reading
an imaginative novel like Ursala Le Guin's (1969) *The Left Hand of Darkness*,
when and if you have the time, and see how that gives you different
insights. Building up this creative capacity can help with the next two
kinds of imagination.

Sociological imagination (Duarte, 2009; Mills, 1959): Think about what it means
to be a member of society, and how the things we do have a role
in how it is shaped. Does an imaginative engagement with the social
world highlight different interpretations? Should you be interpreting
the actions of others as if they have the same advantages or disadvan-
tages as you, or should you try to imagine how their experience of
society is different from yours? Can you think about how others are
affected by the support and endorsement you give to unwritten social
rules? A simple example of these rules is the way dress codes are supported: imagine that an organization is hosting an event to recognize
and thank employees, but specifies "business attire" on the invitation.
Why would you need people to dress up so that you can thank them?
Who is really being gratified in that situation?

Moral imagination (Pless et al., 2022): When your understanding of a situation leads to competing ways of acting in response, both of which
seem morally right, what do you do? A good example of this dilemma
in recent times has been the case of peaceful protests against climate
change in the United Kingdom. Legal officials involved in the trials have
been sympathetic to the reasons for the protests but also feel obliged to
uphold the letter of the law.[2] A growing number of prosecutors found
a way to seek to solve this dilemma by refusing to take part in such
trials.[3] Moral imagination involves looking at a dilemma in which both
obvious options seem equally right – for example, between acting with
compassion or with regard to the letter of the law – and finding some
transformative alternative that squares the circle.

These kinds of imagination are layered and blended in the processes of
reflexive thought, providing ways of enhancing your *contextualization* and
conceptualization (Hibbert, 2021a). Creative imagination – especially if
nurtured – extends the learning from your experience to provide new ways

of understanding a situation. It helps you contextualize what is going on in many ways, rather than going with a dominant model or intuitive answer (bearing in mind my earlier comments about the times when intuition might offer the most appropriate insight). Sociological and moral imagination provide different ways of describing the situation or appropriate action that should follow – they offer you ways to shape a conceptualization that builds on your (enriched) capacity for contextualization, through seeing the world in different ways.

There are a couple of important points that I need to note when thinking about thoughtful reflexive practice and the use of intuition and imagination. The first point is that you will be constrained by time. Although the point of future-oriented reflexive thought is to shape our understanding and guide action in the present, that does not always mean the *precise* moment when an experience strikes you, or when a dilemma becomes obvious. You will need to think about how you can find time for reflexive thought "away from the action", either through introspection or perhaps through writing (Ripamonti et al. 2017). The second point is to remember that even with the benefit of reflexive thought, your understanding will always be limited and "come from somewhere", since experience shapes the way that your mind works (Ripamonti et al., 2017; Sklaveniti & Steyaert, 2020). As we will see in Chapter 5, working with others can give us another way of extending beyond our limitations, but we can still apply thoughtful reflexive practice in our leader work.

Thoughtful reflexive practice and leader work

Thoughtful reflexive practice draws attention to and enriches our capacity to contextualize experience (Collien, 2018; Cunliffe, 2003; Maclean et al., 2012) and, from such insights, develop alternative conceptualizations that help us to understand, think and act differently (Hibbert, 2021a). As we discussed above, the process can involve critical thinking, intuition and imagination and is layered over embodied and emotional insights. With leader work in mind, this pattern of thoughtful reflexive practice is an end in itself, since it is so closely tied to decision making in complex and uncertain situations. However, there are three aspects of thoughtful reflexive practice that have special significance when we are involved in leader work. They involve developing "negative capability", legitimating and supporting imagination (for yourself and others) and care in establishing heuristics. We will look at each of these in turn.

Developing negative capability – and bricolage

The term "negative capability" is a curious phrase, first used by the Romantic poet John Keats in correspondence. What it means is the ability to be in a condition of not knowing, and to be comfortable with that. If you can develop your negative capability, it will allow you to mobilize your intuition and imagination and be more aware of the non-cognitive insights (like emotional perceptions) that you have, rather than trying to overrationalize based on knowledge that is inadequate (Saggurthi & Thakur, 2016). In other words, negative capability means being comfortable with uncertainty and being willing to "fill in the gaps" using something other than our familiar knowledge and ways of going about things. To some extent, this is a lesson that we all had to learn during the COVID-19 pandemic, when the normal rules of life were suddenly torn up, especially in the early days when we could not predict week by week how the future would look. In the face of such intractable uncertainty, negative capability provides the underlying capacity to bring together embodied sensations, emotions and thought, and to do so imaginatively. This is a method that uses whatever is available at hand to the best effect, rather than a careful design process; that is, it involves bricolage (Baker & Nelson, 2005; Steffens, Baker, Davidsson & Senyard, 2023).

The idea of bricolage has been found to be useful in a range of situations where uncertainty is irresolvable, particularly where there is a need to capture a hard-to-grasp opportunity or a need to maintain business as usual through unprecedented challenges. Good examples can be found in studies of entrepreneurship: grasping opportunities is of central importance to entrepreneurs and so it is no surprise to see them acting as bricoleurs. For example, Stenholm and Renko (2016) found that bricolage was essential for the success of entrepreneurial firms. They associated "entrepreneurial passion" as a motivating force but found that the benefits that could be realized from this energy depended on bricolage in the use of available resources, leading to creative solutions to problems and innovative pathways towards opportunities. In addition, they found that where emerging firms included people who were adept in using bricolage in these ways, they were more likely to survive and prosper.

It is also interesting to note, in passing, how Stenholm and Renko (2016) emphasize the emotional – passionate – angle of the process, which lines up with my earlier arguments about the important role of emotions (see Chapter 3). However, is an emotional angle essential for bricolage? Not necessarily. Others have identified how bricolage can inform strategic moves and everyday action in emerging and traditional industries (Corbett-Etchevers & Parmentier-Cajaiba, 2022), public management contexts (Carstensen, Sørensen & Torfing, 2022) and social ventures (Sunduramurthy, Zheng, Musteen, Francis & Rhyne, 2016). It does not solve every problem, though: an important qualification to the use of bricolage was identified by Steffens et al. (2023). They found that bricolage was less helpful when ambitions or challenges were less demanding. This makes sense: in relatively stable conditions with no opportunities to be seized, there should be a focus on optimization and efficiency rather than disruptive creativity. So, it is important to note that if you don't feel the need to use your negative capability (the conditions don't come with irreducible and serious uncertainty), then bricolage might not be the best focus for your reflexive thought. That is why I link the two concepts together so that you can be thoughtful about your practice. It also, perhaps, marks one area of distinction between leader work and the everyday tasks of management. It is only when there is a need for negative capability, to chart a course despite uncertainty, that you enter the core zone of leader work; and if there is enough knowledge to make it clear what should be done, that is the zone of management (Wolfram Cox & Hassard, 2018).

Legitimating and supporting imagination

I identified three kinds of imagination as being particularly useful for thoughtful reflexive practice: creative imagination (Pless et al., 2022), sociological imagination (Mills, 1959) and moral imagination (Pless et al., 2022). Any of these might help to provide ideas in situations where you need to fill in the gaps or work out a new way forward, and so they can inform leadership in action in direct ways. Beyond that, leader work needs to include the legitimation of imagination – giving people license and encouragement to use it – and the recognition that people need to step outside of their everyday work to develop their capacities in this direction. That can and should include engagement with the arts and literature, which resource our interpretive range in encountering the world by helping us to use insights that go beyond our direct experience. That is exactly what we are trying to do through the use of imagination. In short, imagination needs something to work on – and the richer that material can be, the better. Hibbert et al. (2017) noted that research on how the arts and humanities can contribute to leadership development has shown clear benefits in three ways. They first highlight how the arts and humanities can provide richer descriptions of human life in all of its varied contexts, humanizing approaches to leadership in the process (Ciulla, 2008). Second, they explain how great art can provide particularly potent engagements with experience, leading both to more developed interpretive abilities and enhanced capabilities for self-expression (Taylor & Ladkin, 2009). Third, they describe how the cumulative effect of engagement with the arts and humanities over an extended period is a greater capacity for reflection and interpretation of each subsequent new experience (Cunliffe, 2009; Reichard & Johnson, 2011; Sutherland, 2013; Taylor & Ladkin, 2009).

Overall, imagination includes and develops the reflexive capacity to see things differently, which allows you to think about alternative futures for your organization and your own leader work (Curtis & Cerni, 2015; Curtis, King & Russ, 2017). Furthermore, imagination has a key role in supporting a capacity for foresight. The key task is to develop an imaginative, speculative capability while grounding our conjectures in continuing interpretation of what is going on in the here and now, in order to have a disciplined sense of what may be possible (Cunliffe, 2018).

So, you need to ask yourself where you – and those you find yourself called to lead – are getting the material that will feed the imagination. Are you engaging with creative fiction to see other possibilities that go beyond the everyday? Do you watch movies from cultures outside your own, to get different pictures of what society can look like? Do you engage with different religions and philosophies to stretch your moral thinking? Of course, there are different ways to get to the same effects – I am not trying to be prescriptive – and you will want to enjoy your time engaging with the arts as well as feeling that it is resourcing your work! However, as a useful diagnostic, it is worth asking if your workplace conversations ever stretch beyond the boundaries of work and everyday life. And if they do not, how might you change that and encourage and allow more breadth? This is where my final point comes in.

Care in establishing heuristics

If your leader work is associated with a hierarchical role – in short, some people think of you as "the boss" – then you may have influence over thoughtful reflexive practice for others in an unexpected way. That is, you will influence them through the ways they may build their own heuristics (rules of thumb) based on your preferences. Gigerenzer (2008) explains that the personal heuristics of a leader can become the norm for others, whether this is intentional or not, and that it can have unintended consequences. People avoiding the bear traps of a leader's particular personal shibboleths eventually alter the culture of the organization, in ways that may persist even when the leader is gone. For this reason, Gigerenzer (2008) argues that leaders need to be aware of the kinds of rules of thumb they may be communicating and embedding when they express their particular preferences.

So, if you are trying to support and make space for imagination and intuition, there may be ways that your managerial approach is undermining your leader work. For example, if you require extensive and detailed documents before regular meetings (rather than, say, short presentations at the time), you set a strong focus on order and evidence. But, in the process, you also eliminate scope for imagination: no-one has free time for resourcing their imagination, because they are writing and reading a lot of boring documents. The team may also presume you don't value intuition, based on your preference for detailed information. As another example, if you are known for always being decisive then people will be unlikely to take more time reaching a conclusion, when it could in fact be beneficial to do so. Such cultural heuristics, when communicated by leaders, can be more powerful than explicit values and intentions (O'Reilly, Chatman & Doerr, 2021). So, the clue here is to think about the intentional values you are communicating and the possible shadow-side heuristics that go with them. Mostly, this requires you to think about creating an appropriate balance between formal and informal processes (Yang & Yeh, 2023). If you want to support critical, imaginative and intuitive possibilities for reflexive thought, think about where the looser conversations can take place, and how you can demonstrate your own reflexive practice. I would like to sum up this point with another insight from Gigerenzer (2008), who argued that leaders should reflect on and list their own heuristics and decide whether or not they would wish the organization to be guided by them, before they become embedded in the leader's everyday practice and thereby shape the spirit of the organization.

Summary and actions

In this chapter I have shown how thoughtful reflexive practice weaves together a critical perspective on the past that shaped us and an imaginative and intuitive engagement with the future, that uses different ways of seeing and knowing. This leads to more options about how we interpret what is going on in a particular situation, which in turn gives us more options for future thought and action. These insights show how criticality, imagination and intuition have a role in thoughtful reflexive practice and related leader work. If you are looking for ways to begin applying these insights in your leader work, you will find suggestions below.

Explore your situatedness

To help "know where you are coming from" and support critically reflexive thought, begin by describing your upbringing, culture and current community/ies. Just write some brief notes. Then ask yourself what ways of thinking, values and assumptions are "typical" of people with a similar background to you. For example, you might be part of a particular religious faith community (or none), have ideas about the family, hold certain views on government and so on. Then use the *different lens* or *deconstruction* approach to explore whether the values and assumptions that you have been socialized into might be open to challenge. For example, you might use your creative and sociological imagination to think about what your values and assumptions might be if you had been born on a different continent and a radically different level of wealth. What is essential to you, and what is "accidental"? What other ways of thinking are there, and how does that make you feel about your own formation? Don't forget that your body and emotions may well be involved in this self-understanding.

Get familiar with your heuristics

As a follow-on from the first point, it's a good idea to follow Gigerenzer's advice by trying to develop an understanding of what your rules of thumb are. These are the unconscious companions of the values and self-insights that you find easy to describe, and will be harder to spot. Try to notice the default choices you make under time constraints and collect this information over time. It's important not to try to second guess yourself and interrupt your normal intuitive judgment – but in later reflection, you may want to think about how the heuristics you routinely use communicate certain values and assumptions to others.

Resource your imagination

This feels to many people like tough advice when they have busy lives, but I suggest that allowing yourself to trust your intuitive judgment in appropriate situations comes with the corollary that you will need something more creative in more complex situations. I argue that there isn't a recipe for this, but engagement with the arts and literature (ideally in forms that also give you pleasure) is one way to develop more creative scope – especially if this takes your imagination into other social worlds and cultures.

Develop your negative capability

Accept that there will be times of irreducible uncertainty, and that to some extent that is typical of leader work. Knowing that, you can develop your thoughtful, future-oriented, reflexive practice to weave together intuition, imagination and information in creative ways so that you (and those you may be leading) can "go on". As you do so, don't forget that the critical aspect of thoughtful reflexive practice is still available to you. It can be helpful to look back on your patterns of coping with everyday uncertainty to see if there are any assumptions, ideas and heuristics that you want to challenge. You might also notice occasions when it was difficult to be creative when it would have been helpful, and ask yourself why that was the case.

Notes

1 A cultural reference to an idea from the series *Star Trek*, in which a particular race has purged themselves of emotion and adopts a commitment to logic as a way of being.
2 For example, see the report of a judge's remarks here: www.bbc.co.uk/news/uk-england-birmingham-64683048.
3 The news report related to the decision of public prosecutors to refuse to act in such cases can be found here: www.theguardian.com/environment/2023/mar/24/top-lawyers-defy-bar-declare-will-not-prosecute-peaceful-climate-protesters.

5

RELATIONSHIPS AND LEADER WORK

The cunning mirror of another's view

It is impossible to have a perfect knowledge of yourself solely through introspection. And if you don't know who you are, how will you present yourself authentically in your leader work? Although we can develop substantial awareness of ourselves through attention to our bodies, emotions and thoughts – as we have seen in earlier chapters – there is always an unconscious and intuitive system of thought that remains hard to pin down. Relationships can provide us with different ways of seeing and understanding who we are and what we are doing, to help us see this hidden engine of our thoughts and behaviors (Wilson, 2004). Anyone who has had a heated argument with a partner will recognize how surprising – and uncomfortable – some of those alternative views can be. But, of course, differences of opinion are all too common in organizational life, too.

DOI: 10.4324/9781032721507-5

A PERSONAL STORY: NOT THE RIGHT PERSON

I had been appointed to run a troublesome transformation project. It was troublesome because there had been a failed attempt already, which had seen the last project leader moved out of their management post with time to explore other options. If we didn't succeed this time around, it would cost us an important accreditation that we needed to hold on to. It was also an important project for staff because it would have a real (and positive) impact on their working conditions. The stakes were high and some people felt that I was not up to the job – and a few wrote an email, that they signed collectively, to express this opinion to my boss.

I had the backing of my boss, but I was still concerned about how to respond to the people who had no confidence in me and the process. I got an organization-wide, regular communication strategy up and running, so that hopefully I could get my message out to all staff. We needed the confidence of the community. But I also realized – with a sinking feeling – that I would need to bring some of the people who wrote to the boss into the tent, by including them in some of the working groups that were delivering parts of the project. I did that.

I can't pretend that it was always easy in the group meetings. However, I think the people who were negative got to realize over time that I was *not* as hopeless as they thought, and that I really cared about the project and the staff. More importantly for me, I realized that the negative folk had a lot of useful insights about what went wrong with the previous attempt to deliver the project, and what they knew could help make a difference this time around. They cared about everyone in the organization too and became an important part of the process that made the project an eventual success. If I had followed my immediate instinct to keep them out of the process, it would have been a huge mistake. I realized that you don't have to like people to respect them and do good work together.

In this chapter, I focus on relationships with others and how they can help us to develop new understandings, not least about ourselves, and how leader work can be informed by these insights. The chapter has three main sections. The first section considers the insights we gain through relationships, particularly through the key process of dialogue that underpins relational reflexivity. The second section sets out how we can develop our insights and self-understanding through relational reflexive practice. The third section, which is followed by a brief summary of the chapter with actions for implementation, explains how relational reflexive practice can inform leader work.

Gathering insights through relationships

If we are largely steered by intuition and governed by an adaptive, unconscious level of thought (Gigerenzer, 2008; Wilson, 2004), it will be difficult to understand ourselves fully on a conscious level. This is why the views of others, who see our behaviors, can hold important truths that we might struggle to see. We might not like the picture of us that others paint, but these alternative views are likely to illuminate the particular ways in which we are often guided, not by a conscious internal narrative and thoughtful introspection, but by unconscious systems of thought that we struggle to keep up with. From Wilson's (2004) perspective, the stories we tell about who we believe ourselves to be are at best plausible accounts that struggle to capture our non-conscious behaviors and characteristics that are difficult for us to observe. To put it another way, introspection only gets us so far because we can never observe ourselves well enough to develop a complete picture.

So, in some ways, self-understanding needs to be completed through relationships, in which we invite others to describe the person they see us to be. They will draw their own pictures of who we are based on how we act, as well as who we might claim to be. Although this adds an important and otherwise hard-to-grasp element of self-awareness, that does not mean that the levels we have already looked at – embodied, emotional and thoughtful – do not also provide important insights. However, in relationships we find the final cunning mirror, that lets us see ourselves differently, digging below assumptions and behaviors that are so deeply embedded and unconscious that introspection might never reach them. In this way, relational reflexivity differs from the focus on the here and now that predominates embodied, emotional and thoughtful layers of reflexivity (what am I sensing, feeling and thinking right now – and why?). Instead, it can offer new clues that complement the work that we can do through solitary reflexive practice, by drawing attention to our wider context in time and space. For example, in their work on the influence of family life on individuals, Lupu, Spence and Empson (2018) described how influences from our early lives and upbringing could continue to have an effect long into the future and in a range of different contexts. That is, they found that influences from family life could persist into an individual's professional career, even when they might wish to act quite differently.

The relationships that provide the tools for unearthing hidden structures are mostly relationships with other people but, perhaps surprisingly, they are not limited to that kind of connection. For example, Simon (2013) describes individuals as situated within a web of relationships that can include other people (both directly and through different kinds of media) as well as texts. Books that demand your attention and give you a different view of the world may indeed "change your life", but it is not self-help books or scientific studies that are likely to do this. Instead, it is much more likely to be novels and other forms of narrative fiction that have a strong impact on us. Stories are more memorable than other forms of text (Mar et al., 2021), and because they provide characters with whom – while immersed in reading – we form close attachments (Rain & Mar, 2021). Stories also help us to develop our ability to understand and have empathy with others (Mar, 2018). In this way, fiction helps us to develop our capacity for a "theory of mind", to have ideas and insights about the mental states of others (Leverage, Mancing, Schweickert & Marston Williams, 2011). We can turn that "theory of mind" on ourselves, too: a "relationship with a text" may be useful for you as a way of seeing yourself differently, especially if you recognize that character(s) in the story have some similar behaviors to your own.

Seeing ourselves in/as stories

If you find yourself at odds with the idea of a meaningful engagement with fiction, it will be uncomfortable to hear that the stories we create about ourselves are also fictional, at least in part. This does not mean that you are deliberately lying to yourself or others. But because the unconscious and intuitive rules of thumb guide so many of our actions are hidden to us, the stories we tell about ourselves and our choices rely instead on a variety of other sources of which we are more aware. In particular, Wilson (2004) described four alternative sources that we use to make sense of how we (and perhaps others) act in a given situation. The first he describes as "shared causal theories", which can often be expressed in the form of an aphorism or simple statement, offering examples such as "absence makes the heart grow fonder". Basically, in the absence of a more concrete theory to explain our own actions, we turn to our traditions and the common inheritance of culture for an explanation. The second source of explanations he describes is the observation of covariation, for example, if you have runny eyes and sneeze a lot in a flower garden, you will conclude that you have an allergy to pollen (otherwise known as hay fever). The third source of explanations is an idiosyncratic theory that makes sense to you, based on a pattern that may or may not be logical. Think, for example, of the many sporting stars who have superstitious habits that they follow before an event. It is probably not the "lucky socks", for example, that lead to their success on the field. The fourth source of information is our own privileged access to our thoughts, emotions and memories, all of which may provide us with some insight about why we respond in the way that we do in a given situation.

With so much going on in the construction of the stories of ourselves, it can be interesting and useful to see how successful writers craft narratives that produce compelling characters. So, one of the benefits of engaging with fictional characters crafted by skillful writers is that they try to get "under the skin" of their characters, and that sometimes has the benefit of allowing us to see how our own behaviors might come from similar hidden causes. Another benefit is that we may see ourselves differently in relationship to fictional characters, in ways that challenge our assumptions and behaviors. Fictional characters might even include influential role models, where they are seen as moral exemplars. Moral exemplars – people whose values we find appealing and attractive – can exert a profound influence on who we seek to be and how we go about presenting ourselves (Gill, 2023).

I have discussed encounters with fictional characters because many readers will recognize the experiences obtained through reading that I have talked about, and such encounters provide a low-risk way of reflecting on the unconscious drivers of your own behavior. Of course, relationships with "real" others can have unsettling or motivational effects, too. The important point is to consider all the ways in which we receive ideas about ourselves from others, even (and perhaps especially) if they are challenging (Rhodes & Carlsen, 2018). However, as we have already seen in Chapters 2 and 3, embodied and emotional experiences can also suggest insights. Indeed, our emotions may provide another way of challenging the stories we create about ourselves. As Wilson (2004) notes, people are not equally skilled when it comes to being emotionally self-aware. Our privileged internal knowledge, idiosyncratic theories and reliance on traditional insights from our culture can all lead us to think of ourselves in a way that is at odds with our feelings.

Relationships and dialogue: the reflexive reception and resolution of new insights

Despite the potential of relatively safe engagement with stories as a way of seeing ourselves in different ways, other people are likely to offer the best source of new insights. Relationships with other people are the most likely means to radically develop and change our views about ourselves and others because they provide an opportunity for extended and open critical engagement. In this vein, Hibbert et al. (2014) describe a process of "engaging otherness" and "enacting connectedness" that supports the possibility of relational reflexivity. Engaging otherness means seeking out those with different views and experiences from our own. Enacting connectedness means working together to develop some potential for shared meaning, which might be different from either of our starting points. Bohm's (2004) work on dialogue sets out a similar process. His approach is designed to be for any number of people in a group, rather than just two people (he notes that "dia" is derived from a Greek root and indicates "through" and not "two") and is intended to let meaning flow within and around the group. Bohm's (2004) vision is of a non-judgmental process that allows some new understanding to emerge, instead of providing an adjudication between two or more competing positions.

While relational reflexivity can be understood as a kind of dialogic process, it is one that is inherently complex, somewhat unpredictable and rather troublesome (Bissett & Saunders, 2015), and conflict or confusion can arise if people are engaged on a deep level. Similarly, Bohm (2004) acknowledges that conflict may arise within the process he describes when fundamental assumptions and commitments emerge in the dialogue. In addition, I suggest that the overlaps with interconnected embodied, emotional and thoughtful aspects of our experiences and self-understandings also come into play, some of which are harder to see (as I have discussed in earlier chapters). This means that even though relational reflexivity has a basis in non-judgmental dialogue, it can feel like a struggle at times. The struggle is likely to become more apparent the closer we get to our fundamental assumptions, when the critical insights of others begin to challenge and reshape an understanding of ourselves to which we may be deeply attached (Larsson & Knudsen, 2022).

Relational reflexivity therefore involves *receiving* a lot of new insights, concepts and possibilities, without any confident expectations that it will be easy to accept them and reshape our understanding – especially of ourselves – around these new ideas. Indeed, in our everyday lives we may have developed forms of practice that are focused on avoiding anything that requires us to change in some fundamental way (Hibbert et al., 2019), and this resistance can obstruct learning and change. The possibility of habitual resistance means that the process of *reception* of new ideas needs to be followed by a process of *resolution*, a back-and-forth conversation to work out how the puzzles and contradictions that come with challenging ideas can be resolved (Hibbert, 2021a). Building a shared way of seeing – a shared "interpretive horizon" – is the result (Gadamer, 1998; Hibbert et al., 2017). We build a connection through an overlapping but not identical understanding with the person from whom we received the new insight. However, the final part of the resolution only happens when the insight becomes knowledge that is *applied* in our future practice (Gadamer, 1998). Thus, resolution is a process that considers our emerging knowledge as the basis of connections and possibilities in general terms, but it also considers how the new knowledge might transfer to other contexts, and what its effects might be (Chilvers & Kearnes, 2020). Only then might we feel able to change our lives in response to it.

The need to consider application applies to new knowledge about ourselves because of our situatedness: we can have different ways of behaving and being in different contexts. Think, for example, about how you interact with people at home or in a social setting, compared to your place of work or study. Thus, understanding our situatedness draws attention to the fact that multiple relationships may be in play in our lives in different ways – some form a troublesome aspect of the context while others are connections providing helpful insights. At this point it is important to state something that should be obvious: we cannot assume that all relationships will be helpful, or even neutral. For example, reflecting on a key moment in her career, "Jane" explains the effects of relationships in this way:

> Relationships were a central feature of the situation; however, it wasn't until others [in this authorial team] pointed this out to me that I realized how central they were. The situation arose because of an unhealthy relationship with a colleague; my initial blocking behavior was an attempt to resist other colleagues' behavior with whom I also had relationships with. And, then it was another relationship with my then Department Head that prompted me to start looking for options to fix the situation ... I've often believed that the relationships I have with a few close colleagues are what make the difference in the [teaching and research] work we do, but by seeing reinforcing relationships as a practice, I can see that those relationships provided a way for me to move out of a difficult space without leaving the organization ... I kind of feel like I worked through it [the difficult situation] rather than running away from it.
>
> (Hibbert et al., 2019, p198)

Because of all the complexity involved in gathering insights through relationships, we need to consider how relational reflexive practice can be developed in helpful ways to navigate a course. In doing so, we need to bear in mind that: we will struggle to identify and describe our own behavior, because of the role of our unconscious and intuitive systems of thought; we can connect with both texts and other people to help challenge our assumptions and stories; and relationships are not neutral, since some may be supportive sources of insight while others are problematic. Accordingly, I now go on to consider the kinds of reflexive practice that can be helpful, with all of those points in the background.

Relational reflexive practice

Relational reflexivity is centered on the ways that we *receive* new ideas about ourselves (and the things we are interested in) and *resolve* the confusion or resistance that these new ideas generate. Building on these core ideas and the caveats that I set out above, there are three ways to go about developing relational reflexive practice. The first is to engage in dialogue with trusted others. The second is to connect with "textual conversation partners", sufficiently rich books that allow you to see yourself differently in relation to characters and situations in the story. The third is to blend aspects of these two approaches together, by sharing autobiographical notes with others for interpretation and as a basis for conversation. I explore each of these in turn below.

Dialogue

Engaging in dialogue is something we already do, to a degree, quite naturally. The majority of people have at least a few trusted friends with whom they share their troubles and from whom they seek advice. In our working lives these relationships are often pair-wise (rather than the large dialogue groups described by Bohm, 2004). Dialogue with trusted friends can help us get through difficult situations or provide supportive routes for informal learning about, say, the organizations we work in (Beech, 2017; Corlett et al., 2019; Gilmore & Kenny, 2015). So far, so good: but these relationships tend to be founded on similarity and common interests, so they may not provide as diverse a range of perspectives as we might wish, if we wish to see and understand differently. Friends are also unlikely to tell us things about ourselves that we might find really uncomfortable.

In contrast, some argue that if you want feedback on the unconscious behaviors that you would otherwise struggle to acknowledge, then a stranger might be able to describe those just as well as a friend. In addition, a stranger might be less reticent to do so, when the description might affect your feelings (see Wilson (2004) for an extensive discussion of this). The point is that almost everyone can notice behavior, and we are all used to interacting on the basis of what we see people do and how we interpret it. However, while inviting comment from unfamiliar people may help us to know ourselves better, setting up a mechanism for working with strangers might be quite complex – especially getting sufficient observation time to allow the relative strangers to form opinions. One way around this issue is to use video recordings of interactions, which can allow the observer to both tell and show what they see. For example, Ajjawi, Hilder, Noble, Teodorczuk and Billett (2020) describe how the use of video allowed a group to develop their collaboration through being relationally reflexive about their interactions.

However, there is a fine balance here, since it can take people some time to "behave naturally" with strangers, and formal and situational constraints can mean that we do not necessarily reveal much of ourselves in everyday situations. This is part of the reason why team-building events often involve unfamiliar situations, activities and locations – the normal rules are less apparent, and people may behave differently toward each other. There is value in supporting different forms of interaction, and also having diverse connections that bring different perspectives with them. I encourage you to develop relationships with an edge of unfamiliarity and difference, if there is interest in relational reflexive practice on both sides. Regardless of how and why relationships are formed, to enable a balance of support and challenge there needs to be some basis of trust, and that is normally developed over relatively long periods of time. Hibbert, Beech et al. (2022), for example, described how the process of developing trusting relationships, in order to be open to the insights of a partner in dialogue, could take years.

With the background to dialogue (finally) in place, how do you go about it? One way is the pattern described by Bohm (2004). His process begins with participants sharing opinions, seeking to do so without hostility and without defensiveness about what has been shared. The intention is to generate ideas that others can add to as they are "passed around" the group in the form of collective thinking, rather than embarking on a mission to persuade others in the group about the rightness or usefulness of an idea. Bohm's (2004) idea of dialogue is a process for relatively large groups that are trying to overcome tensions within or between communities, and it is worth reading his classic book to find out more about that. However, it has some principles that I abstract, adapt and apply more generally for setting up dialogue on a smaller scale (including between two people). My adaptation of these ideas works in this way:

An imprecise starting point: The starting point for the dialogue can be (and perhaps should be) quite vague. For example, you might simply be interested in learning about yourself and your relationships. As an example, see Korber, Hibbert, Callagher, Siedlok and Elsahn (2023), who worked to understand their own pattern of friendships.

Flow: The conversation should be allowed to flow from a loose starting point and go wherever it will, rather than being tied down to a specific starting point or limits.

Vulnerable openness: Our own behaviors and opinions should be included as part of the conversation, recognizing that there is a degree of vulnerability in this and exercising appropriate care in response to that exposure (Hibbert, Mavin et al., 2022).

Clarification not contestation: As assumptions about ourselves become apparent to others they should be open to challenge, but they should not usually be defended. Instead, further inquiry to try to resolve the impression another receives about us could follow (Tell me more ...; When and how do you notice that ...).

Conclusion: The conclusion of the dialogue could be a set time, or instead when participants feel that it has concluded.

For the purpose of relational reflexive practice, the dialogue does not have to result in common ground, neither is there a requirement for either participant to simply accept their conversation partner's views. However, it should lead to a situation in which each participant has had some assumption(s) challenged and has material for personal reflection that can build on that. While there need not be common ground there should be a sense of a "shared interpretive horizon" (Gadamer 1998; Hibbert et al., 2017) – participants then have a better (though not perfect) understanding of how each other sees things and some insights about how their interpretations do and do not overlap.

This process I outline can seem like an idealized rational conversation, but it is important to remember that our bodies are not "taxis for our brains" and that we will be present as embodied and emotional individuals (even if via online meeting systems, as is increasingly common). This can bring difficult challenges for those of us who feel that we are perceived as different in ways that bring particular (unconscious) reactions from others. For example, Adjepong (2019) talks about her experience as a researcher working in a particular community in the United States, and the ways that her embodied presence as a queer black person led to reactions from the community. While her experience was at times emotionally distressing and uncomfortable, she felt that her physical presence helped to reveal the community's ways of thinking and opened up unexpected possibilities for connecting with them. One of the main points that Adjepong (2019) makes is that our embodied selves are also "read" or "heard" in certain ways, and that impacts how possible conversations of a more conventional nature might flow. This can show up troublesome assumptions but also make different patterns of connection possible (see also Callagher et al. (2021) for similar insights). Others have also emphasized the point that we bring our bodies and emotions to relational reflexive practice, and that connection with others necessarily involves *all* aspects of ourselves (Nichols, 2009; Keevers & Treleaven, 2011; Rhodes & Carlsen, 2018). For these reasons, despite the current ubiquity of online meeting technologies, I suggest that dialogue for reflexive practice is best conducted in person whenever that is possible.

Reading as conversation

The second approach to relational reflexive practice, engagement with "textual conversation partners", is obviously a more flexible process and does not even need to be deliberate. The books that you choose for your everyday reading will provide more or less potential for a relationally reflexive experience, depending on whether they are very easily digested forms that require little focus from you or something that requires more imaginative engagement. As I have already noted, the most useful texts are likely to be novels, since stories are memorable as well as providing characters that we can relate to (positively or negatively) and, for these reasons, research has shown a link between this kind of reading and empathy (Mar, 2018; Mar et al., 2021; Rain & Mar, 2021).

In general, reading novels (and engagement with other forms of art) can provide a rich encounter with the "human condition" in ways that might otherwise be inaccessible to us (Ciulla, 2008). In addition to developing some immediate insights, engagement with literature can also help us to develop our interpretive capability (Hibbert et al., 2017; Taylor & Ladkin, 2009), equipping us with a cunning mirror for examining ourselves along with a more powerful lens for observing others. Both of these benefits can make us a better partner in situations of dialogue, where there is a wish for open generative learning, in a spirit of curiosity (Hibbert et al., 2016). Becoming an "experienced interpreter" can also mean that when we return to familiar and favorite texts, we interpret them differently, developing new insights (Weinsheimer, 2004).

My advice for using "textual conversation partners" as part of your relational reflexive practice is relatively simple and non-directive, and hopefully encouraging. Read novels that include voices and situations that are distinct from your own, and that require some imaginative connection from you. Most of the classics would qualify – but so would, for example, well-written detective fiction set in another period of history or in a location very different from your own, or science fiction. All you need to do is enjoy your reading, provided that it shows you other views of life.

Interpreting stories

The third approach to relational reflexive practice is a process that has formed the heart of my recent research with colleagues (see, for example, Hibbert, Beech et al., 2022). In small groups, we share short, written stories of incidents or extended experiences where we feel we encountered emotional or practical struggles in our working lives (and these incidents have often been leadership situations). Our experiences are written up in a form that can be shared so that all can contribute a story, and these stories are passed around the group for critical interpretation. This involves everyone adding marginal comments and questions, after which we meet (perhaps several times) to talk through and resolve the insights that come from this process. The quote from my pseudonymized friend "Jane", that I shared earlier, is one example of where this process leads.

It may be helpful to show another example in more detail, to see how the process begins as well as where it leads. What follows is one of the stories shared in another recent research project, about the vulnerable leadership experiences of senior university managers (Hibbert, Mavin et al., 2022). The details in the story have been anonymized and generalized so that no individual is identified – this is a disguised and composite picture that summarizes a range of individual experiences:

> "Dave" was suffering with severe mental illness, failing academically and far away from the prospect of a qualification of any kind. We were running out of academic and support options. Should he leave the university? All of the right professional reports were provided, so I was well informed. But I also knew that the mental health support outside the university was extremely limited. He had self-harmed to the edge of suicide in the past, been taken to hospital and treated. Then discharged at 3am – just turned out to find his own way home – on the basis that he had been assessed as "not at risk". What happens if the university team is not there to pick up the pieces? The thought that

occupies my mind, as I make the decision, is that we are keeping him alive in the hope that he may recover. No-one else is going to take care of him if we don't.

But bending the student progress rules (again), so that I can keep Dave safe, would mean asking specialists and general staff to work with someone who is likely to engage in extreme self-harm, someone who could make more than one suicide attempt ... and may be successful. I have seen the harrowing effects of experiences of student self-harm and suicide on staff, and those effects are severe. Some people have left their careers after that kind of experience. Some I have met on campus still ... but see the haunted look of someone who was once so happy-go-lucky. And I know, I surely know, in the pit of my stomach that my choices can lead to that. So, I realize that my decision about Dave involves choices about how many people are going to be hurt and in what way. I cannot prevent all harm. If I protect Dave – someone whose education and treatment are both failing – I will most likely move the harm on to others. I also feel sure that I am going to feel pain, either way. There is no way out of that for me.

(Hibbert, Mavin et al., 2022, pp11–12)

Working with others helped to show how the writer could better understand themselves. The process of sharing and interpreting the story revealed the dark, unconscious and seductive attraction of the idea of power in such situations: the writer was relying on professional advice and clear principles (suicide prevention being absolutely paramount) and, in reality, had little real choice about how to act. However, the process also confirmed that the idea of responsibility and a burden of moral emotion in these situations felt absolutely right. Some experiences and decisions, however constrained, should hurt, if we are the caring and humane people we imagine ourselves to be. The process also showed that, in such situations, being able to share stories with others who are compassionate provides essential support.

Using this approach to unpack difficult experiences requires a lot from the participants in the process. The relationships need to be open, compassionate and trusting but this must be balanced with a willingness to interrogate assumptions (Cunliffe, 2003) and to be comfortable with having your idea of yourself challenged and changed in a process of collective reflection (Gilmore & Kenny, 2015). The participants may also benefit from having built up their interpretive ability through reading, as I noted earlier, since that can elevate empathy. Furthermore, the skills to contribute to the process of interpretation also need to be balanced with a willingness to hear challenging perspectives, so that learning can flow in all directions. Your assumptions and self-image may both end up being challenged and reframed in this kind of process and it will be uncomfortable, doubly so if you focus on emotionally challenging experiences in your shared stories. However, if you can work through the emotional difficulty of the process then you may generate insights that could be useful for you and for others, who may well recognize and relate to the stories (Beets & Goodman 2012; Ramsey, 2008). In ways that echo the potential benefits of engaging with literature, sharing and connecting with each other's stories can also help us to know *ourselves* better and help us to change (Hibbert et al., 2019). As an additional benefit, this kind of process can also help us to build up our skills in the practice of dialogue *outside* of this structured approach:

> Evidence for the role of dialoguing in all the narratives was most clear in the process of sharing our interpretations of each other's experiences. For all of us, the role of trusted others was integral to this practice and clarified through later rounds of interpretation and response. Dialoguing was an under-developed practice in the stories that we narrated for each other, but the process of interpretive engagement allowed it to flourish. Developing insights through this practice, therefore, took (often extensive periods of) time. In our cases, it took some years to fully explore our experiences and potentiate changes in management practice, through later engagement with others.
>
> (Hibbert, Beech et al., 2022)

Relational reflexive practice and leader work

Overall, the three processes for relational reflexive practice can help us to understand what is going on in and through our actions, and form a better understanding of who we are. However, we need to be aware that this will involve confronting some unconscious, intuitive aspects of ourselves that are intimately involved in our personal make-up, to a much greater degree than we might expect. These are important challenges that can inform leader work, if we are willing to be vulnerable in ways that allow us to learn, change and grow.

The challenge and necessity of vulnerability and relational reflexivity

I need to be clear that taking a vulnerable, learning perspective on leader work is not a mainstream stance and it is somewhat countercultural. Recent history has shown the old model of strong (and to be frank, unfeeling and immovable) leadership continues to persuade large sectors of the population, as the persistent fascination with charisma and heroic leadership continues (Fourie, 2023; Jan Verheul & Schaap, 2010; Parry & Kempster, 2014). My view is that the brutality in political leadership that this "taste" has allowed to develop is devastatingly bad. Furthermore, a model of strong, unbending leadership involves a lack of self-awareness and capacity for compassionate judgment, which should rightly be seen as fundamental flaws in an individual's moral character (Hibbert & Cunliffe, 2015). It is, in short, toxic leadership (Smith & Fredricks-Lowman, 2020). You might take a different view, but to be honest I would be surprised you have read so far into this book if you do.

It is also important to point out that developing your approach as someone capable of vulnerable leader work might not be the easiest way to have influence or get things done. It can involve situations that cause considerable emotional stress for yourself (Hibbert, Mavin et al., 2022) or require you to be a toxic handler for others as you absorb and deal with all of the negative emotions and views that seem to be endemic to most organizations (Frost & Robinson, 1999). Furthermore, the necessary reflexive practice is challenging, as I discussed earlier in this chapter and in the previous chapters: working with our bodies, emotions and thoughts is clearly demanding, before we even get to the complexity of working with others. However, this is also an approach that supports a rehumanization of what leadership is about, and provides the potential for leader work to be developed in ways that support that aim (Petriglieri & Petriglieri 2015). It is also consistent with popular characterizations of more ethically informed and caring leadership styles, such as servant leadership (Mittal & Dorfman, 2012) or authentic leadership (Algera & Lips-Wiersma, 2012).

Ethically informed approaches require us to know our moral values, and have an idea of who we are and where we are coming from. However, that is not necessarily straightforward, and people can expect different things from leaders in different contexts (Sydow et al., 2011). In addition, the ways of presenting ourselves that will seem persuasive can vary as new situations develop (Parry & Kempster, 2014; Petriglieri & Petriglieri, 2015). Particular situations can lead us to different behaviors or make different possibilities from our repertoires of action more salient and appropriate (Wilson, 2004). An awareness of situational influences does not mean that we will be shifting our fundamental values in the moment, but we do need to have a better understanding of the range of actions and narratives that our values support. Most lived patterns of ethics are consequential, after all: we will react differently depending on the people involved in a situation and the outcomes that may affect them. What is inescapable in all of this, though, is the need for us to still have some coherent sense of who we are, despite the fact that aspects of ourselves might be pushed to the foreground or background depending on the situation (Callagher et al., 2021).

Developing coherence: the multilayered stories of ourselves

Most of us have an idea of who we want to be (or not want to be), thoughts about the kind of actions that becoming (or not becoming) that person requires of us, and how we embrace or resist change in order to end up being the kind of person that we wish to be (Hibbert et al., 2019). These ideas can motivate, to some extent, what we choose to do. Thus, Wilson (2004) explains that we can be motivated by different ideas about who we might become in the future: the person we would like to become, the person we feel we ought to be and the person that we might be afraid of becoming. Wilson (2004) also explains that the problem with these imagined selves is that they are not the only motivation for our behaviors and choices. Our unconscious works a lot more quickly most (or perhaps all) of the time, and the unconscious drives may not be the same as the conscious stories we create.

The work I laid out in earlier chapters to engage with embodied experiences (Hardy & Hibbert, 2012), emotional perceptions (Hibbert, Beech et al., 2022; Hibbert, Mavin et al., 2022) and intuitive forms of thought (Gigerenzer, 2008) may provide some traction on the systems that operate more rapidly than our conscious thoughts. Those approaches generate a lot of useful insights that help us to see how our initial interpretations of situations (and/or our role in them) might not be the full story. However, the insights they bring still face the risk of being "sanitized" to fit with our preferred ideas of who we are and wish to become, and they don't necessarily help us to build a coherent picture of ourselves that integrates the unconscious with the conscious. We are always looking through our adaptive unconscious and telling ourselves about it in consciousness after the fact (Wilson, 2004). Relational reflexive practice helps us to find a way through this conundrum, by providing us with outside observations of our behaviors that we can compare with our preferred, conscious stories of ourselves. The key point is to bring these multiple sources together meaningfully, by constructing a narrative that draws on all of these sources of insight and brings them into a coherent whole. As Wilson (2004) notes, with luck this kind of narrative will include at least some aspects of the non-conscious thoughts and feelings that drive us.

We can improve on the "luck" that Wilson (2004) refers to by using relational reflexive practices, such as dialogue and conversations with literature, to surface views of our behaviors to integrate into our personal narratives. I suggest that you actually try to write your personal narrative down and, if you are brave, share it with trusted friends for the "interpreting stories" process (Hibbert, Beech et al., 2022) that I described earlier. This will help to show if there is still some "sanitization" going on in the story. When the story is as honest and comprehensive as you can make it, there may still be some discordant elements – the conscious (desired) narrative may be at odds with the unconsciously driven behaviors that (observers have persuaded you) are true for you. For example, here is a note from my own reflexive diary:

> I have long considered myself to be an introvert, who through the necessity of leadership roles has had to learn to "act" in an outgoing way over the years. However, recently, when I have shared this self-impression with others it has been met with disbelief. They recount experiences of seeing me being quite extrovert, and seeming to take pleasure in it. Maybe I have acted so much that my behavior has changed this aspect of my personality?

In fact, Wilson (2004) argues that a process of "faking it till you make it" can actually change our adaptive unconscious, so it's quite possible that a commitment to "pretending" to be an extravert can lead you to become one; in that way, a conscious motivation for solitude comes to be at odds with the non-conscious motivation for social engagement. This example leads me to set out the choices you have when aspects of your story seem to be inconsistent. When there are discrepancies between how you describe yourself, your behaviors and motivations, and what others notice from observing what you actually do, there are three choices. You can either change the conscious narrative about who you are or what you do, work on changing unconsciously driven behaviors that you find undesirable, or a little of both. Developing a more coherent narrative in which your conscious and non-conscious motivations are aligned has specific benefits for leader work (we will turn to that in a moment) but it also supports better wellbeing (Wilson, 2004). In general, the more aligned your conscious and non-conscious goals are, the better it is for you.

The potential for greater wellbeing is important given the emotional burden that vulnerable leader work can entail (Hibbert, Beech et al., 2022; Hibbert, Mavin et al., 2022). However, there is another reason why a coherent self-narrative can be important for leader work. That is, it helps to avoid the risk of being seen as a hypocrite, if your self-narrative and espoused motivations are at odds with how you actually behave (Treviño & Brown, 2004). Importantly, having a coherent idea of self needs to include your "personal life" as well as your "working life", since it seems that you cannot separate your role from your person in the eyes of those who see how you behave in a variety of contexts. For example, Bush, Welsh, Baer and Waldman (2021) found that perceptions of an individual both as a moral person and as a moral leader (in the execution of their official role) had an influence on the attitudes and behaviors of others in the organization.

In many organizations there may also be sets of "organizational values" that managers and leaders espouse allegiance to. If others in the organization notice an individual's behaviors are at odds with the espoused values, then they will regard this as hypocrisy and may form a negative view about the organization as well as the individual (Cha & Edmonson, 2006). Organizational values provide an easy standard of comparison for behaviors, and having an available standard of this kind makes hypocrisy easier to spot (Greenbaum, Bardes Mawritz & Piccolo, 2015). Believing that someone is a hypocrite also brings further doubts about the future and an individual's security within it. Greenbaum et al. (2015) found that when employees felt convinced that a leader was a hypocrite, they felt that the leader's behaviors in the future were unpredictable, and in the face of this uncertainty and lack of trust some were motivated to leave the organization.

The overall point of relational reflexive practice for leader work is to really become who you say you are. That may require you to take on board some hard-to-hear lessons and think about how you might change your behaviors in order to shift your unconscious motivations, or alternatively require you to be more realistic about what really drives your choices and actions. However, even when your self-understanding feels relatively coherent, it may be tricky to express your identity and have it recognized by others as you would wish. That requires identity work, which is the focus of Chapter 6.

Summary and actions

In this chapter I have shifted from a focus on how we interpret what is going on to draw more attention to how we interpret who we are and how we struggle to know ourselves fully. Despite the insights we can draw from embodied, emotional and thoughtful reflexive practice, addressing this question effectively requires relational reflexive practice. Through dialogue, conversations with literature and interpreting our stories of ourselves, we can engage others in relational reflexive practice, to help us surface the non-conscious motivations and assumptions that may be at odds with the stories about ourselves that we construct. For all of us there is value in developing a coherent self-understanding, to support our everyday wellbeing as well as our leader work. If you are looking for ways to begin applying these insights in your leader work, you will find suggestions below.

Think about your reading habits

I am glad that you take an interest in non-fiction texts, for obvious reasons! However, the work of Mar and colleagues at York University has shown that reading novels can help us understand the different mental states of others, which can provide a cunning mirror for our own behavior as well as help us to be empathetic and insightful partners in dialogue. So, you might want to include a variety of types of reading in your practice, which includes non-fiction for new knowledge and fiction for new (self-)understanding.

Develop connections with other reflexive practitioners

The point about relational reflexivity is that it is founded on relationships with others. With one notable exception (mentioned in the next point), this means making connections with other people that you can trust to be both compassionate and critical. You may find the right kind of connections within workplace friendship groups (Korber et al., 2023), but you are most likely to find the right sort of engagement with others who – like you – are developing as reflexive practitioners who draw insights from their own experiences and exchanges with others.

Engage in dialogue

"Conversations with texts" will only take you so far, so you need to jump in and engage in dialogue. I have set out loose guides for two ways of approaching this (a conversational approach and an approach based on interpreting stories of difficult incidents) in this chapter, but you don't have to stick with either. Any conversation that allows others to challenge your explanations and assumptions is likely to be helpful. The only essential point is to remember not to try to defend your opinion (especially about your own behaviors), but instead to find out why your dialogue partner thinks differently. What have they seen that you have not?

Write and rewrite your personal narrative

Keep using processes of dialogue to identify the differences between your conscious and non-conscious motivations, and be prepared to rewrite your personal narrative to bring the two closer together. That may involve some difficult work to change some behaviors, but having a coherent sense of self is likely to make your leader work more effective. You may still have to vary what you do as different situations may demand that, but a coherent sense of self that unites conscious and non-conscious motivations will help you to develop within a consistent and compatible repertoire – and avoid undermining your position through being seen as a hypocrite.

6

IDENTITY WORK AND
LEADER WORK

Is identity obvious?

If you are interested in *leader* work, why should you be concerned with *identity* work? For some, identity can be tricky, confusing, disrupted and displaced. Reading about the experiences of others makes this clear. For example, Mahmoud Darwish's (2011) poetic autobiography *In the Presence of Absence* shows how identity is a difficult subject if you have been a refugee. However, in contrast many of us presume that our own identity is a simple thing. We feel confident that our sense of who we are is obvious to everyone around us. But this confidence is brought into question when we think about the multiple identities that we may have in our collection: I think here of my own range, which includes professional, ethnic, family identities and more, each of which can be more or less meaningful in different situations. Knowing our range of identities can help us to see that there is work involved in expressing each one of them when we feel that it is important to "be ourselves", as the story below suggests.

DOI: 10.4324/9781032721507-6

A PERSONAL STORY: A REVOLVING CLOSET DOOR

My position on support for young trans people is unequivocal. I have seen enough anguish, heartache and self-harm when they experience rejection and contempt from former friends, unsupportive parents and even members of the public who take pleasure in hate. Trans people are more likely to suffer from abuse, discrimination and suicidal intentions than any other section of the community.

I realized, in a senior management team meeting, that my own identity needed to be expressed in my support for trans people too. I am a gay man who looks like any other average middle-aged white male. Even though I was one of the first people to be visible on the organization's LGBT+ role models web page, I appear to others under a cloak of assumed averageness most of the time. At one particular meeting, discussion was proceeding on fairly muted terms about what should be done in response to transphobic messages that were circulating in our community. Some people were voicing an opinion that there were free speech issues, and that supporting trans rights cut across other people's interests. It was as if I was not there. So I had to say: "For me and others in the LGBT+ community, trans rights are human rights". I was really uncomfortable about having to do so.

To be fair, the senior management team were generally caring and thoughtful people, and my comment did have an impact on the conversation. So, the abiding question was not about the issue we were debating, but the way in which my identity had been important but somehow invisible. The thought I was left with was: do I have to *keep* coming out, or wear rainbow clothes or something?

In this chapter, I consider how we seek, and struggle, to express the kinds of identity we wish to espouse when we feel it is important for us. I connect that challenge to leader work, in three sections. The first section considers identity work and the threats and challenges that this form of work responds to. The second section sets out the importance of identity for leadership, and the types of identity that can support influence in organizations. The third section, which is followed by a brief summary of the chapter with suggested actions for implementation, explains how identity work is an important and intrinsic part of leader work.

Identity work

Are others *really* convinced by the identities we seek to present? Or do they question and challenge our identity, perhaps to the extent that we lose the ability to present it, or choose to suppress it deliberately? This is where theories and debates about identity work are helpful in shaping our understanding about how coherent identities are achieved and presented, despite challenges. What researchers who focus on identity work mean by the term is:

> a process through which people strive to establish, maintain or restore a coherent and consistent sense of self. In the face of potential disruptions of, or threats to, their identities, people seek to salvage their sense of self by resolving tensions and restoring consistency.
>
> (Beech et al., 2016, p506)

Identity work is, then, about the things we do when engaged in presenting, communicating or defending our sense of self in our interactions with others (Alvesson & Willmott, 2002; Beech, 2011). Consider, for example, how we use the things we say, the way we dress and our everyday actions to communicate our sense of self, sometimes through almost staged-managed performances in particular organizational settings (Brown, 2017; Conroy & O'Leary-Kelly, 2014; Perrott, 2019; Riach & Cutcher, 2014). Consider, also, how we might present ourselves quite differently in our work settings, families, social circles and so on (Ladge, Clair & Greenberg, 2012). What this means is that both the sense of self we are seeking to present and the way in which we present it (or perform it) can vary in different settings. These variations arise because different aspects of who we are become more or less meaningful in different settings and relationships, and our sense of self may change over time. The end result is that responding to external and internal changes requires different kinds of identity work in different times and places, in order for our sense of self to be coherently presented and defended.

Because of all the complexity involved, the identities that we construct are not always experienced as coherent and resilient, even by ourselves. Instead, our identities (and/or how they are accepted by others) may feel quite precarious (McGivern, Currie, Ferlie, Fitzgerald & Waring, 2015; Petriglieri, Ashford & Wrzesniewski, 2019). This sense of a precarious identity may be more likely to arise when we are faced with uncertainties.

The experience of precarious identity constructions, and difficulty switching between different presentations of ourselves, are much more likely when the boundaries of the situation are uncertain or unclear and the relationships we have with others in that context are also rather vague (Beech, 2017). The outcomes of our identity work may also be more precarious when identity threats exceed our capacity for shoring up and strengthening our self-understandings and how we present them (Alvesson & Willmott, 2002). There is only so much you can do to express yourself in a hostile environment. Thus, to understand what it is possible for us to achieve through identity work, we need to think about how it is both stimulated and undermined by particular challenges and threats.

Identity challenges and threats

Importantly, as we all know, others have their own assumptions and interpretations about the kind of person that we are, and snap judgments can be formed very quickly. This means that others' views will constrain or enable the kind of identity we can successfully present, and therefore influence the kind of identity work that we use to respond to their views. For example, think about how a seemingly straightforward identity like "father" faces a whole set of cultural assumptions, personal experiences and different interpretations from family members (Hibbert, 2021a, pp76–77, 82–83, 136). There is plenty of scope for confusion and accidental incoherence around even a seemingly simple identity. Individuals can face direct identity threats, too, and good examples of this are highlighted by Callagher et al. (2021), who recount how their identities as researchers were undermined through discrimination:

> *Viktor*: The three of us, me, Claire and Craig – the industrial partner who organized the gig – were standing in front of some fifteen managers from local companies. Being informal, as usual, Craig went on about our contributions to the day, weaving some news and politics into his comments. When attempting to make a point about me, a foreigner being involved in research on some local co-operatives, he looked at me and asked: "what boat did you get off?" The room went dead silent.
>
> *Claire*: We were invited to a half-day of strategic events that started with an Annual General Meeting and then a strategic session.

There were about 50 people and were told in advance that people would be interested to know who we are and would be welcoming. Before the first session, between the sessions, and after the second session, there was a lot of networking, and as we were told to expect, a number of people came up to introduce themselves and find out who we were. While talking, it was suggested we talk to an older man who was well-known in the area. When the older man passed us, the person I was talking to waved him to join us and introduced me as a researcher. The older gentleman replied that he was known as "the godfather" of the industry, that he was happy to see a new lady in the district, and had a son looking for a wife if I was interested. My sharp reply saying if only I wasn't married played to his gendering of my identity.

(Callagher et al., 2021, pp449–450)

Thus, our sense of self can often be less than robust and at risk from threats. However, some experience of identity threat, tension and confusion is always intrinsic to identity work, since without such challenges there would be no need to "shore up" constructions of the self through forming and repairing them in our acts of self-presentation (Brown, 2015). It is important to distinguish, though, between the everyday level of challenge and the more radical and difficult threats that prevent us from fulfilling our purposes for self-expression.

Identity threats are difficult and disruptive when they prevent individuals from supporting, for example, professional or role identities, as the earlier examples from Callagher et al. (2021) show. In such cases we might seek to respond to identity threats in protective ways. We can do so by highlighting particular distinctions and values, as in the quotation from Claire above, in which she resists gendered assumptions. Alternatively, we might restructure our presented sense of self by adapting our identity or by changing the practices that are involved in self-presentation (Ahuja, 2023). Another insight from Callagher et al. (2021) provides a good example of adapted self-presentation. They describe how researchers who were worried about how their accents identified them as non-locals sought to find out about the "backstories" of their research participants. This information included the participants' education and professional interests but also their personal networks, hobbies and other interests. The researchers used this information to be able to engage in conversation that was more connected

to the participants' interests and daily lives, which made them feel less concerned about their accents. Effectively, they crafted a "temporary identity"
which connected with the participants on some shared level, while pushing other aspects of themselves into the background.

However, when individuals feel that their identity – where this is closely
held or valued – has been invalidated, or when the threat invokes irreconcilable tensions (where resolving the threat to one valued identity characteristic would involve undermining another), then the necessary identity
work may be out of reach or feel ineffective (Beech, 2011; Beech et al.,
2016; Ellis & Ybema, 2010; Grimes, 2018; Sveningsson & Alvesson, 2003).
Difficult or irreconcilable tensions of many kinds can be experienced, especially when different social contexts overlap or collide. Examples of such
difficulties include tensions between work and family identities, problems
in representing or enacting conflicting organizational or personal values,
experiencing troublesome contrasts between team and professional identities or handling multiple and conflicting institutional rules and norms
(Cain, Frazer & Kilaberia, 2019; Carollo & Guerci, 2018; Ladge & Little,
2019; Shams, 2019).

Identity work challenges in organizations

The main goal of identity work is a sense of stability and coherence, to be
sure of who we are and communicate that to others. However, in organizations people engage in identity work for other reasons, too – for example,
to support or challenge organizational goals or influence others in their
organization (Grimes, 2018). Identity work in organizations is also associated with particular challenges, as well as particular purposes. There are at
least three kinds of particular challenges that can be a concern.

The first challenge is the way in which performance is assessed in organizations, which can interfere with how we would naturally use identity
work, in favor of presenting ourselves as someone who fits the measures
that the organization chooses to use (Knights & Clarke, 2014; Shams, 2019).
For example, Lindebaum (2017) explains how individuals working in a
chain of coffee shops are expected to present a positive, upbeat personality to customers at all times. Along with explicit and disturbing identity-
related measures of that kind, those in formal leadership positions can
inadvertently set the cultural tone (Gigerenzer, 2008) and this can lead to

implicit expectations about behavior, dress and even appropriate non-work activities. When such expectations flip over into explicit requirements, the result is a tyranny of taste in which normal self-expression is curtailed.

The second challenge arises when professional status or values are undermined, which has a knock-on effect for the ways in which people are able to offer ideas, opinions and insights that holding a particular professional identity would normally allow (Grimes, 2018; Kyratsis, Atun, Phillips, Tracey & George, 2017; McGivern et al., 2015). Good examples in this case are: the professional freedom of expression that journalists and scholars expect; the need for scientists to be able to speak about their research evidence and findings; and the ability of clinicians to direct care in ways that have the patient's best interests in mind. A good example of how problematic undermining professional values can be, related to clinicians, is described by Gigerenzer (2008). He recounts how a doctor did not administer a particular test that could confirm a disease, because it could only give choices that increased the patient's anxiety without offering viable treatment options. The doctor's judgment was based on the view that this test result could only, therefore, decrease the patient's quality of life for several years through anxiety. The patient sued the doctor for not administering the test, although that decision was based on his clinical judgment. The patient won the case. As a result of the ruling, the outcome is that in the United States, some clinical organizations may prefer doctors to administer every possible relevant test, even when that may be detrimental to the patient's wellbeing, since failing to do so may risk litigation. Clinicians may, therefore, find themselves advising some test and treatment options, even if it they are at odds with their judgment of the patient's best interests (and thereby at odds with their professional values). Recognizing how broken this is, Gigerenzer's (2008) conclusion is to shift clinicians to a different kind of identity work – a family relationship and not a professional one – when seeking advice: you should ask your doctor what they would advise for their mother, not what their recommended treatment options for you are.

The third kind of challenge arises when organizations recognize some identity categories and not others, leading to some members of the organization having the experience that they feel misidentified (Meister, Jehn & Thatcher, 2014). I had an experience of this myself, when taking on a senior administration role at a university while still remaining active in research and scholarship. After a while, some faculty colleagues suggested that I could not understand their work because, since I was a member of the senior management team, I "was not an academic". Similar concerns arise when some aspects of personal identity are not recognized, or are even actively discriminated against. It is still the case that in organizations (and in society at large) some people do this to bolster their own self-image at the expense of the "other", for example, through promoting stereotypes which diminish the comparative status of their victims (Koveshnikov, Vaara & Ehrnrooth, 2016).

Identity threats of this kind can be particularly difficult and disruptive when they prevent individuals from supporting their professional or work role identities, by pushing a non-work identity characteristic into the foreground and stigmatizing it (Fernando, Reveley & Learmonth, 2020; Lee & Lin, 2011; Wesley, 2002). This kind of discrimination drags identity work away from the professional domain where people may be seeking to focus, and also undermines an individual's integrated sense of self. The bigot's intention is to achieve one or both of two things. One aim may be to imply (or even state) – wholly against any logic – that being someone of a particular gender, ethnicity or sexual orientation is incompatible with a particular professional identity. The other aim is to make the discriminated individual become so occupied with defending aspects of their non-work identity that they have no capacity to support identity work focused on their role, so that others do not recognize them as the professionals that they are.

Overall, individuals in organizations are likely, at some time or other, to experience difficult identity-related conflicts, tensions or other forms of threat. The identity work we do to respond to these challenges when they arise is hard, since such experiences affect us deeply, in emotional as well as practical ways (Winkler, 2018). Thus, it is important to recognize (if it was not already obvious) that emotions are central to effective identity work and not a mark of failure (Muhr et al., 2019; Soini & Eräranta 2023).

Responding to identity threats and challenges

If emotions are normal in the experience of identity threats and challenges, they can also be key to responding to them, in three ways. On one level, people may learn to "live with" identity threats through finding emotional support through friends and colleagues (Meister, Sinclair & Jehn, 2017). On another level, people may seek to work on neutralizing their emotions themselves, by trying to develop a "thick skin" or sense of "numbness" to the angst and pain that identity threats bring (Shepherd & Williams, 2016). Alternatively, on a third level, people may try to protect the part of themselves that feels emotionally vulnerable to identity threats through suppression – the at-risk identity is pushed into the background, where that is possible, through compartmentalization (Kennedy-Macfoy, 2013; Perrott, 2019; Shams, 2019), while at the same time a robust identity presentation might be built on resources from a less threatened identity position (Brown & Coupland, 2015).

Compartmentalization of certain aspects of our identity can feel like a diminishing and isolating strategy. In addition, all of the three approaches for responding to identity threats mentioned above are relatively passive. They do nothing to "turn off" the source of challenge. Furthermore, dealing with identity threats through actions like compartmentalization can distance us from certain identities in the eyes of others, preventing connection with those facing the same challenge. Thus, compartmentalization, in particular, risks cutting off the potential for collective visibility and mutual support (Kane & Levina 2017). This leads to the loss of collective resources to support more adaptive or threat-resistant responses to identity challenges.

Other approaches to responding to identity threats can be more active, and lead to stronger forms of resistance to the challenges that we experience. These are often connected to moral emotions. One of the most obvious forms of resistance is supported by the formation of collectives, who can resist identity threats through positive identity work that challenges stigma. For example, Jammaers and Ybema (2023) describe how a community of performers with dwarfism engaged in a range of responses to identity threats that included deliberately provocative and shocking forms of identity work to express pride in their distinctiveness. The collective response to identity threats described by Jammaers and Ybema (2023) centers on the moral emotion of *pride* and its expression through highly visible public activities. Similarly, we will all be familiar with LGBT+ Pride marches, parades, festivals and cultural events. These all have exactly the same purpose, which is to support identity work which resists (and sometimes even inverts) stigmatization.

The connections between identity work to handle identity threats and patterns of moral emotions illuminates why emotion regulation is difficult for those attempting to support a particular position in organizations, including a leadership role, through resistance (Sirén, He, Wesemann, Jonassen, Grichnik & von Krogh, 2020). Moral perspectives can also be important for responding to identity threats in more subtle ways. In addition to the positive expressions of particular identities within a collective, through mobilizing the moral emotion of pride, individuals may recognize others as presenting morally desirable identities that can be patterns for adaptive approaches. That is, if a person with a desired identity is showing moral characteristics through their identity work, they may be seen as a desirable role model. Gill (2023) explains how these moral role models can influence identity work through stimulating moral emotions, promoting reflection and providing conceptual resources and examples.

However, adaptation – collectively or individually – is not necessarily an easy way to respond to identity challenges. It will depend on two things: whether – and how much – someone feels that the threatened aspect of their identity can actually be changed, and how they value or attach special importance to that particular aspect of their identity (Meister et al., 2014; Meister et al., 2017). Sometimes people can adapt and reconstruct their identity in other ways, by enlarging their understanding of themselves rather than pruning or reshaping selected aspects (Barker Caza, Moss & Vough, 2018; Beech, 2011). Think about what happens when someone moves from a front-line professional role to a managerial one, say, from a practice-focused nurse to a clinical manager. It is likely that the professional identity is still there (and essential for credibility with the teams being managed) but it is part of a broader mix, encompassed within the idea of being a manager. Another example that may resonate for some is the change from being a spouse to a parent. The spouse is still there in the larger role that family life brings, and it is probably important not to forget that.

Building on the idea of identity reconstruction it is possible to go further, by seeing an identity challenge not as a threat but perhaps as an opportunity to develop a new idea (or understanding) of yourself that you find appealing. Both the transitions to manager and parent, mentioned above, might be seen in this appealing, positive way rather than just as an "enlarged" conception of the self. Positive, opportunity-framed change might happen through building on experiences of responding to threats over time, to develop a complex, future-oriented narrative (Ahuja, Heizmann & Clegg, 2019; Jonason, 2019). This kind of story construction helps to support a clear sense of *desired* identity/ies while at the same time resisting threats that force us into an *undesired* identity construction (Barker Caza et al., 2018; Costas & Fleming, 2009; Ellis & Ybema, 2010; Sveningsson & Alvesson, 2003). Having a coherent and persuasive story about who we are (becoming) takes us part of the way, but for an identity challenge to be flipped into an opportunity, there must be something hopeful that becomes visible, some prospect of an appealing future that fits with our story. If a hopeful future-oriented narrative is possible, it provides a sense of positivity about the self going forward (Petriglieri et al., 2019). Hope is the crucial element here. Bataille and Vough (2022) argue that when individuals are able to develop a sense of hope by reconstructing identity challenges as opportunities and not threats, they are able to think more broadly and creatively about the possibilities that are open to them. Similar insights have been suggested by Conway, Tugade, Catalino and Fredrickson (2013).

The conclusion is that some identity challenges can be turned into opportunities, if we have grounds for hope and can think creatively, especially through the construction of new future-oriented self-narratives. I will discuss the role and importance of narrative more extensively in the concluding chapter of this book. For now, I will simply point out that an "opportunity framing" of identity threats could also apply in the contexts of leadership, although there are some specific challenges and opportunities that apply in those cases.

Leadership and identity

Identity is a key issue for effective leadership. If how we are seen in the eyes of others is always the somewhat precarious outcome of identity work, that certainly applies to whether and how we are seen as a "leader" (Carroll, 2016). Going further, how we are seen also affects if and how we are able to lead – if you are not perceived to fit with the expectations of what a leader is, you may find it difficult to be effective (Fourie, 2023). However, what is meant by a leader identity is open to different views and perspectives, and is contingent on a variety of factors.

One of the important factors affecting the possibility of a leader identity is how you understand "leadership" yourself. That is, how you construct your own rules of thumb about what the term means will influence how you feel able to express an identity as a leader (Day, Harrison & Halpin, 2009). Your understanding is likely to be based on your experience and interpretation of the actions of others you recognize as leaders. This experience of interpreting and recognizing leadership builds up into your own "implicit leadership theory" (DeRue & Ashford, 2010). Thus, it is unsurprising that people may reflect on whether or not they are currently a leader based on their interpretations of others and their degree of personal alignment with their interpretation of them in the here and now (Zaar, Van Den Bosche & Gijselaers, 2020). They may also evaluate their possible role as potential leaders based on their scope for constructing future-oriented stories that align with those of the people they see as role models (Jonason, 2019).

Whichever way we come to understand leadership, a leader identity is not likely to be the only one that any of us has. Are you a leader while at home making lunch for your kids, or taking part in a Spanish class or trying to get a new personal best on a 5 kilometer run? Moreover, from the identity work perspective, even in an organizational context the leader identity is only really "there" when it is expressed in a particular situation. None of us is a leader, for example, when we are dealing with routine correspondence or taking uncomplicated decisions. For most people in organizations, a leader identity sits within a more expansive identity and pattern of activities as a manager (Alvesson & Sveningsson, 2003; Sveningsson & Larsson, 2006). This often leads to difficulties when someone takes on or is promoted into a new role, in which the activities and identity of a leader suddenly become meaningful. Yip, Trainor, Black, Soto-Torres and Reichard (2020) build on the research of Hannah, Jennings, and Ben-Yoav Nobel (2010), Hammond, Clapp-Smith and Palanski (2017) and Miscenko, Guenter and Day (2017) to develop some key insights in this area. They describe how people assuming a formal leader role, such as military officers in their first command, can find their leader identity troublesome. Over time the struggle is resolved, as the leader identity grows in strength and is better integrated with other identities that the individual considers important for them. However, events and interventions can mean that the leader identity can still vary in strength over the long term, as individuals continue to make sense of it in their changing contexts.

As the work of Yip et al. (2020) suggests, there is no guarantee that someone who is "expected to be" a leader can simply express that identity. There are complex internal and external challenges that shape the possibility, even when these do not take the form of clear identity threats. As well as the challenge of integration, another important factor is how others in the organization (or any other setting for leadership) limit what is possible as an expression of leader identity. That is, alongside the possibility of everyday identity threats and challenge, leaders also experience identity *regulation*. Identity regulation means that the scope for identity work and the kind of leader self-identity that can be expressed might be constrained by established norms in the organizational or contextual culture (Sveningsson & Larsson, 2006). Think, for example, of political leadership; it can be executed in a variety of different modes and styles (Lees-Marshment & Smolović Jones, 2018) but there is often an expectation that the leader must behave in a way that appears strong rather than weak, aligned with a kind of macho, uncompromising stance in a heroic mode (Schedlitzki, Edwards & Kempster, 2018).

Overall, expressing a leader identity is always a complex achievement because it involves both personal challenges such as integration alongside social and relational aspects, which introduce contestation about what is allowable as a leader identity (Yip et al., 2020). This does not mean that the "allowed" leader identities are just those that fit the genuine interests of members of organizations or society, and there can be undesired outcomes instead. For example, followers may desire and regulate expressions of leadership along heroic lines, but that does not mean that their interests will be respected by those with the "muscular" leadership styles that they have enabled to take charge (Driver, 2013, 2015; Fourie, 2023; Schedlitzki et al., 2018). Having enabled someone who exhibits "strength" rather than "weakness", it should not be a surprise when the leader feels that their strength allows them to take actions in ways that may be at odds with what is expected. Indeed, Fourie's (2023) review concluded that as long as someone fits with the expectations of "what a leader looks like" for the collective, they can get away with paying little heed to the actual interests of their enablers. Sadly, recent experiences of political leadership – such as those seen in the United Kingdom following the Brexit vote and the COVID-19 crisis – seem to align with this insight.

While some political leaders have been able to get away with extreme behaviors, thankfully the normal pattern in everyday organizational life is more constraining, because expressing a leader identity means engaging with complex intrapersonal and interpersonal challenges. To tackle such challenges, people can engage in development activities to overcome some of the difficulties they have in strengthening and expressing their leader identity (development activities that this book is intended to explain and support, as you will have noticed). But such development processes need to include a focus on two alternative integration choices that help the individual, who is struggling to express a leader identity, to select appropriate development pathways and opportunities. The first option is to aim for the leader identity to be the main form of self-expression. This is likely to be the pathway for those who find, whether their self-understanding is contested or not, that they strongly associate with a leader identity (Hammond et al., 2017). That strength of association may be due to particular competencies or abilities, or vice versa: you may need to be able to express the identity in order to be able to use your abilities. The ability to use acquired knowledge and skills in leadership contexts is inherently tied to how others accept and/or recognize the potential for you to enact the identity of a leader (Ahmadi & Vogel, 2023). Thus, as with any form of identity work, this is not simply a matter of individual choice: a leader identity is likely to be more strongly held when it is also recognized by others (DeRue & Ashford, 2010).

The second option is to integrate a leader identity alongside other valued identities – to feel that it is a part of who you are but not a dominant part – and become more comfortable in using identity work to switch in and out of the leader identity when a role or context demands it. This requires some thoughtful reflexive work to accommodate the leader identity and its meaning comfortably, alongside other valued identities (Van Knippenberg D., Van Knippenberg B., De Cremer & Hogg, 2004). However, this is essential for shared models of leadership as well as being able to act straightforwardly as a manager, which will be the appropriate identity for the majority of everyday tasks (Alvesson & Sveningsson, 2003; Wolfram Cox & Hassard, 2018).

Overall, the choice of development pathway associated with becoming more confident in the identity work associated with a leader identity depends on what you believe that to be. People may experience a leader identity in a variety of ways. This may stretch from one fully integrated extreme in which people believe themselves to be a leader in everything they do, through to a more fractured position at the other extreme in which people believe themselves to be a leader only in one particular context, along with possibilities for partial integration between these extremes (Hammond et al., 2017; Zaar et al., 2020). From the point of view of someone committed to reflexive practice – someone who is always learning and changing, and open to the possibility that others can sometimes provide different and more useful insights than our own – the partially integrated view makes the most sense. This perspective also aligns with how people have been shown to handle the difficult transition process in developing a leader identity that may be experienced when promoted to a new role or joining a new organization. Both the partial integration view, and the difficulty of transition, point to the experience of being "betwixt and between" – existing in a liminal condition – when having to develop or express a leader identity in a new context.

Being caught in an uncertain and unmapped transition process between a clear understanding of your previous role and the need to express a new, coherent leader identity is a struggle, in which the new context becomes an identity workspace (Petriglieri & Petriglieri, 2010; Yip et al., 2020). Within this workspace leader identities may be aligned and integrated with other valued identities in ways that lead to a coherent expression and internal understanding (DeRue, Ashford & Cotton, 2009; Ibarra & Barbulescu, 2010), or the new and old identities may simply clash, at least for a while (Amiot, de la Sablonniere, Terry & Smith, 2007).

If developing a leader identity involves contested identity work, choices about integration and liminal processes, we are clearly looking at something that is a rather tenuous achievement. Indeed, Lees-Marshment and Smolović Jones (2018) argue that a leader identity is malleable and can be "undone" through changing the practices and language that are used to support it.

Taking this tenuousness and malleability further, there is an argument that a leader identity (and the identity work that supports its expression) is associated with practices – the small-scale things that people do in organizations and society to connect meaning and action – rather than formal roles and structures. In this vein, Wolfram Cox and Hassard (2018) see leadership as intrinsically related to practice[1] and as a task that involves identity work, in a situated context with others, in its execution. In some ways this is easy to understand, based on the everyday experience of certain identities.

Think, for example, of what happens in the average university classroom. A lecturer needs students to be engaged with her in the context of a lecture in order to successfully enact the role through identity work. This is a fact that has caused a lot of existential angst amongst academics, in the post-COVID-19 age of recorded lectures and empty lecture halls. Similarly, all leaders need others (followers, or perhaps collaborators) to be engaged with them in order to be able to enact leader work in practice. This means that the term "leader" needs to be understood as a fundamentally relational identity (Petriglieri & Petriglieri, 2015), tied to particular practices that constitute leader work. That realization should make the identity of leader less heroic and more open to challenge, in most organizational situations and roles. But as we have seen, there are plenty of popular heroic (or populist despotic) ideas about what a leader is that can cause people to miss these nuances, and instead have simplistic and idealized notions about what a leader can do. Thus, Wolfram Cox and Hassard (2018) note that to avoid these dangerous oversimplifications we need to acknowledge and discuss how leadership experiences can involve uncertainty and troubling emotions because of their relational, situated character and the irresolvable tensions that leader work sometimes involves. With all of that ambiguity and anxiety in mind, we now need to consider what we can actually do, through the use of identity work, to make leader work possible and effective.

Identity work as leader work

Here we enter the difficult transition from what we know about leaders and identity work to what we might do in practice. While there are no precise answers, there are two particular strands of leader work that build on and use identity work. Taken together, they can enable you to develop a coherent sense of your identity possibilities so that they include the identity of leader, and to know how to present a clear leader identity that is both true to who you are and recognized by others. Each of these aspects is covered in turn below.

Developing coherence: integrating reflexive practices

Much of the groundwork for coherence comes from the reflexive practices covered earlier in Chapters 2 to 5, that covered embodiment, emotions, thought and relationships. Taken together, reflexive practices that cover these areas can help you feel more "at home" in your body, better able to respond to emotions, more aware of the benefits of reflective thought and able to realize the benefits of exploring the limits of your (self-)knowledge through dialogue in relationship with others. Much of the focus of such reflexive practice is to develop inner coherence and self-understanding. But that coherence also becomes visible and plays out in our leader work, and becomes most apparent in forms of identity work.

Embodied reflexive practice

As discussed in Chapter 2, the different kinds of signals we experience in our bodies have important effects on the way our emotions are experienced, how our thoughts take shape and influence how we interact with and understand other people. Embodied reflexive practice helps us to show congruence – to use body language that is aligned with the confident and/or calm disposition that we are seeking to communicate through talk (Palmer & Crawford, 2013).

Emotional reflexive practice

Chapter 3 explained how emotions can affect us immediately, in a particular situation, or affect us later through evoked memories. In either case they alert us to some potential information about a situation and ourselves that it is worth gathering, taking care as we do so as to avoid the traps that firing up the wrong response can lead us to. Emotional reflexive practice helps us to be aware of the value of the emotional messages that we send and receive, and may help us to legitimize and weave emotional aspects of stories into our leader identity.

Thoughtful reflexive practice

I explained in Chapter 4 how thoughtful reflexive practice weaves together a critical perspective on the past that shaped us (Hibbert et al., 2010; Hibbert & Cunliffe, 2015) and an imaginative and intuitive engagement (Elbanna, 2015; Gigerenzer, 2008) with the future that uses different ways of seeing and knowing. In this way we have more options about how we interpret what is going on in a particular situation, which in turn gives us more options for future thought and action in a range of situations involving uncertainty. One of the primary attributes that people will look for in a leader is that they make it possible for others to feel confidence in a collective way forward (Ganz, 2010). Thoughtful reflexive practice helps us to be aware of the irreducible uncertainty that is present in most contexts and helps us to be able to take decisions and act anyway, through the right use of intuition, imagination and bricolage. Demonstrating these capabilities can form part of leader identity work.

Relational reflexive practice

Relational reflexive practice helps us to focus attention on how we interpret who we are, and how we struggle to know ourselves fully. Through dialogue, "conversations" with literature and interpreting our stories of ourselves, we can engage others in relational reflexive practice, to help us surface the non-conscious motivations and assumptions that may be at odds with the stories we tell. Our ability to tell a persuasive story of ourselves, implicitly or explicitly, is going to be strongly connected to effective leader identity work. As I will explain later, the story needs to connect with the preferences of the organization or social group on one level, but it also needs to be an authentic expression of who we are.

Table 6.1 provides a summary of the benefits of the different forms of reflexive practice for identity work. The labels of *congruence, care, consideration* and *conversation* may be helpful in remembering the benefits of the levels in day-to-day practice.

Table 6.1 Reflexive practice benefits for identity work

Reflexive practice level	Role in identity work
Embodied	*Congruence:* feeling and presenting the impression of being "at home" and at ease in your body
Emotional	*Care:* being alert to the emotions of yourself and others, and how that affects how we perceive each other
Thoughtful	*Consideration:* mobilizing thought, intuition and imagination to be confident in the face of uncertainty
Relational	*Conversation:* being aware of the gaps in our self-knowledge, and developing insights from talk and texts

Presenting a recognized leader identity

All of the preceding discussion risks leading to the inference that there is one "magic" leader identity that we need to be able to establish through identity work. That is obviously not the case, but research has shown that there is something that all readily accepted leader identities tend to have in common. That is, individuals who are most easily accepted as leaders are also likely to be seen as "prototypical" members of the organization, or the dominant group within it, that they lead (Empson, Langley & Sergi, 2023; Fourie, 2023; Gleibs & Haslam, 2016; Ullrich, Christ & Van Dick, 2009). This means that they strongly exhibit the core attributes and behaviors of the relevant profession or industry, so they are seen as an ideal member of the organization. Think, for example, of the behaviors and attributes you might expect from the leader of an accountancy firm, a hospital or a social media company. You can probably outline some quite different expectations relatively quickly.

An exception to the prototype rule is that organizations in crisis may appoint external, non-neurotypical leaders to "shake things up", but they will likely have to use tough tactics that involve conflict to do so (Gleibs & Haslam, 2016) and the "outsider" will find that their leader identity is not accepted easily. So, one key aspect of identity work for a new leader to be aware of is to think about whether they are aligning with more consensual, prototypical expectations or have to take on a conflictual position. Either position may be appropriate, depending on the circumstances. There may still be nuances in identity work in either case, too, because different groups across a complex organization may have different ideas about the ideal prototype, and offer different kinds of identity challenge or threat in response.

Beyond the prototype model – the dimension of ingroup fit – there are many ways of enacting identity work in ways that fit with a consensual leader identity. Individuals still have personalities and varied identity portfolios, after all, and different kinds of organization may involve different kinds of action and interaction. For example, Lees-Marshment and Smolović Jones (2018) show how politicians use identity work flexibly, to adopt a number of positions that present different kinds of leader identity that are appropriate for particular contexts, processes and purposes. Their research showed a range of identities that focused on consulting, boundary spanning, wise judgment or self-assurance and authority. The types of leader identity observed in Lees-Marshment and Smolović Jones' (2018) study might not be expected to be seen in their precise forms outside of politics, but they do show that a range of expressions are possible. Generalizing from their insights, we can see some common variations that might be possible in other kinds of leadership situations, along two dimensions. The first is the authority spectrum, ranging between collaboration at one end and control at the other. The second is an engagement range, stretching between connecting and boundary spanning at one extreme and a kind of judicial independence at the other. Yet, underlying all of the identities described by Lees-Marshment and Smolović Jones (2018), you can still see the traces of a prototype ideal citizen, and it is not unusual to see politicians describe themselves as a "woman/man of the people". Leader identity work therefore includes discovering how people in the organization or social group understand themselves, so that you can explore how you might genuinely represent aspects of their desired prototype, and explore different forms and expressions of that prototype, through varying identity work to suit the different contexts and situations in which you need to act.

Changing identity norms

It is important to point out that the prototypical leader identity that is most easily recognized by the members of an organization could be exclusionary. The very fact that there is a prototype is likely to indicate bias (Fourie, 2023), and discrimination of various forms can get in the way of many kinds of professional identity work (Callagher et al., 2021). Thus, leader work may involve crafting new and more inclusionary narratives that allow different aspects of identity to be accepted, so that you can challenge bias. Since those perceived as the "ultimate insider" are likely to be endorsed even when they are acting unfairly (Ullrich et al., 2009), they also have the opportunity to act more positively by using their freedom of action in a constructive way. Somewhat paradoxically, it is being able to express the identity of the "ideal insider" that gives someone the ability to challenge and change bias. Fourie (2023) argues that recognized leaders who are seen as the "ideal insider" are "entrepreneurs of identity", and they can bring about change through supporting a wider, superordinate identity that stretches across different organizations, or by recognizing multiple identities. Over time, the recognition of multiple identities can allow a much broader set of people to be seen as "insiders", because there are more categories with which they can connect and therefore be recognized more easily as leaders in their turn.

Leader work therefore involves not just *enacting* different kinds of identity work personally, it also involves *sponsoring* different kinds of identity work in response to the identity threats that may be experienced by others in the organization. One form of sponsorship is to support responsive approaches that counter stigmatization of identities (Fernando et al., 2020; Lee & Lin, 2011; Wesley, 2002) through public expressions of pride (Jammaers & Ybema, 2023). Another is to bring forward those who might otherwise be excluded, as moral role models (Gill, 2023). Perhaps the most powerful approach, however, is to craft a narrative that takes the organization into the future in a unified way. I turn to that final piece of the leader work puzzle – crafting personal and collective stories – in the concluding chapter.

Summary and actions

In this chapter I have reviewed the idea of identity work, and shown how people in organizations and social groups need to engage in this form of work to defend their sense of self against threats and challenges to their identity expressions. Against this backdrop, a leader identity is built on our own implicit leadership theories, may take time to develop and emerge and can either be integrated as the dominant sense of self or as one of many personal identities. I advocate the second perspective, based on the fact that leader work is only meaningful in certain situations and contexts, and we likely have more mundane aspects of our lives too. Moreover, seeing a leader identity as one among many helps us to avoid developing an unrealistically heroic picture of ourselves. Building on these insights, I have explained how reflexive practice that supports leader work also supports identity expressions through developing congruence, supporting emotional flexibility, enabling intuition and imagination and allowing us to work on a coherent story of ourselves with others. Finally, I have outlined how using our inner self-knowledge and understanding of the context can help us to express and support a leader identity that will be recognized and allow us to act. If you are looking for ways to begin applying these insights in your leader work, you will find suggestions below.

Use reflexive practice to support coherence

Before you can confidently express and defend your identity, during leader work or in other contexts where an important identity from your portfolio is in play there is an essential first step. You need to know who you are, and be comfortable with that. The reflexive practices developed and aligned to leader work in Chapters 2 to 5 can help (see the summary in Table 6.1). While this will help you to have a coherent story about yourself, that does not mean you will have a single integrated identity that suits every context. Instead you will have a portfolio that will be important to you (for example, parent, Belgian, non-binary, accountant, athlete) that make sense in the different scenes in your story.

Develop an understanding of the "prototypical person"

Since organizations and groups expect a leader to be the epitome of a group member, you will need to understand how group members see themselves. If you have been a member of the group or organization before leader work is expected of you (perhaps through a promotion) then you may already have an intuitive idea about this. Maybe that accountant identity is the one? However, you may want to spend some time listening and observing if you have to do leader work in a context that is new to you. Can you soak up the cultural cues that people use in their identity work? Can you connect with and use these cues, authentically, in your own identity work?

Consider identity threats and challenges in the context

It may be the case that "fitting in" as the prototypical group member will not work easily for you because of identity threats. These may include various forms of discriminatory behaviors, of subtler preferences for particular kinds of experience, preferred professions or group expectations for cli-chéd leadership behaviors (a psychopath can end up as a leader through "charm", for example[2]). If the culture is discriminatory you will want to influence and promote change, but you will first need to protect your leader identity, and other identities that are important to you, through using the passive or active methods of countering identity threats discussed earlier in this chapter.

Use identity work deliberately, as part of your leader work

Identity work is intimately tied up with leader work because people are influenced by who they believe you to be as much as by what you say. This may involve more than simply developing a "leader identity", which, as we have seen from Lees-Marshment and Smolović Jones (2018) can take a variety of forms. Instead, it could involve mobilizing a professional or personal identity. There may also be issues on which you are called to lead where expressing a personal identity can be powerful, provided it fits with your coherent self-narrative and supports the impression of your integrity (Palmer, 2009). This includes challenging bias through sponsoring different forms of identity work for others, so that what "fits" with a recognized leader identity is reconstructed to exclude only one kind of behavior: namely, discrimination.

Notes

1 See Raelin (2016) for a rich discussion and more fundamental view of *leadership-as-practice*.
2 See   www.forbes.com/sites/victorlipman/2013/04/25/the-disturbing-link-between-psychopathy-and-leadership/?sh=212b5b4e4104 for a discussion of this.

7

CONCLUSION

LEADER WORK STORIES

Narrating a way forward

Once you know who you are, what must you do? The focus of previous chapters has been how leader work involves inward and outward forms of work, largely involving reflexive practice and the practice of identity work. Although both of these forms of practice will have cumulative effects, there are times when more specific actions are needed. In particular, leaders are expected to be guides in conditions of uncertainty (Ganz, 2010). To provide this guidance, leader work requires attention to two particular tasks. The first task is to craft two kinds of stories: individual stories that provide a more extensive grounding for our self-awareness and identity work at key times; and collective stories about the future that help the organization to navigate a way forward (Ganz et al., 2023; Shoup & Hinrichs, 2021). The second task is to remember that we need to continue to adapt as circumstances change, and we need to help the organization to adapt, too. This task involves recognizing that our personal self-development is a continuing process (Hibbert et al., 2017), as established in the opening chapter of

DOI: 10.4324/9781032721507-7

this book. For that reason, we need to avoid being trapped within a static story of our own creation. That recognition can help us to balance "writing" personal and organizational stories with "reading" new insights about ourselves and the world, through reflexive dialogue, to inform change.

A PERSONAL STORY: FROM NARRATOR TO PROTAGONIST, AND BACK AGAIN

I was working with friends on research about reflexive practice after emotional experiences. We had all shared stories of incidents in our careers that we had found difficult. I thought the story I shared, having mulled it over far too much for years, was one that I knew inside-out. Yet one of my friends retold the story in a way that made me see my own role in the incident in quite a different way. It was a revelation.

I have since found it really helpful to narrate my *future* plans to the same friends – describing how my choices might play out in my career – before committing to major changes. Over time, I also found that I could also (in a very loose way) imaginatively explore what they *might* say about a particular choice, without discussing it with them. I may still take a decision that is at odds with the actual or speculatively imagined views of my dialogue partners, but I feel much more confident about my choices when our views align.

These insights make it something of a risk in sharing stories from my own career in this book, as I have done in every chapter. You are now one of many additional dialogue partners, forming your own views about my choices and the kind of person that I am. Those views will influence what you make of the main ideas in this book.

The two key tasks – crafting stories and connecting "writing" with "reading" through reflexive dialogue – keep leader work in balance. Crafting stories supports the development of enough confidence about who we are and what the organization is, to be able to take decisions about how to act when the future is uncertain. Reflexive dialogue prevents that confidence from slipping into overconfidence, by alerting us to different ways of seeing things and helping us to see when change is needed. This also helps you to realize that in some situations, the only thing that you can change is yourself and your role in the story. In the following sections I look at these two balanced tasks in detail, before offering some concluding thoughts on leader work.

The power of narrative: crafting stories of the future

In earlier parts of this book, I have alluded to the importance of narrative, especially in relation to relational reflexive practice and identity work in Chapters 5 and 6. This section connects with, reinforces and develops those points through a concerted focus on narrative itself, and through exploring the connections between stories in organizations, our personal stories and leader work.

Stories in organizations

The terms narrative and story are often used interchangeably in studies that focus on organizations. However, Orr and Bennett (2016), following Feldman, Skoldberg, Brown and Horner (2004), explain how the word narrative is sometimes used to denote an overarching theme that connects many stories within an organization. In such cases the overarching theme describes a general direction of change or development, like "growth". Narrative in this sense does not have all the features that we expect from a story, but still shows some change over time and identifies the driving forces – forces which parallel key figures in a conventional story – that explain the direction of change. Although some forms of narrative might not have all of the structure that is typical of the beginning-middle-end form of a well-told story, as Orr and Bennett's (2016) work suggests, my approach is to use the terms story and narrative more or less interchangeably, as many others do (Garud, Dunbar & Bartel, 2011; Schedlitzki, Jarvis & MacInnes, 2015; Shoup & Hinrichs, 2021).

Not all stories need to be complex, and it is not necessary to deliberately introduce stories in organizations for them to appear in some form. We can all probably recount key incidents in our organizational lives that somehow get passed on as micro stories. Think perhaps of some encounter with frustrating bureaucracy, or conversely some unexpected flexibility when someone was kind by bending the rules. People share their experiences of such incidents, especially when they involve the actions of someone involved in leadership, and these micro stories can accumulate into an overall story that describes the organization. That accumulation may or may not be helpful, and so Shoup and Hinrichs (2021) argue that leader work should include crafting more deliberate organizational stories, because otherwise accidental and incidental micro stories – along with gossip, hearsay and rumor – can accumulate without challenge, resulting in an organizational master story that has a life and influence of its own.

Thus, it is not surprising that there has been a lot of interest in stories in organizations, highlighting how important they are. Examples include: Schedlitzki, Jarvis and MacInnes' (2015) research on how classical stories can be used as resources for leadership development; Dailey and Browning's (2014) analysis of repeated stories in the cultural life of organizations, highlighting how such stories may be received in a variety of ways; Garud et al.'s (2011) treatment of the role of narrative in organizational learning, specifically as a way of preserving experience that can be adapted in new circumstances; Vaara and Tienari's (2011) work on the role of narratives in the reshaping of organizations through supporting the resistance or acceptance of change; Borins' (2012) work on public management, which explored how narrative was key to the contested development and dissemination of management innovations; and Kroeze and Keulen's (2013) work on stories as invented traditions, that leaders develop and use to strengthen particular impressions about an organization. Thus, overall, there is a rich body of material that shows how stories can be important for the preservation of acquired resources from the past, for supporting change and for developing an overarching narrative about the organization and its purpose. In such ways, stories provide a key bridge between the past and future in organizational life. For all of these reasons, Shoup and Hinrichs (2021) argue that if we look for them, we will find that stories in some form are present in all organizations. This leads to another alternative to deliberately crafting new stories to shape the organization's culture and direction: it may be possible to mobilize, adapt or build on existing stories. One might do this by selecting and amplifying either those stories that best support the current direction or those that help to underpin the future-oriented narrative that helps to point to a new way through uncertainty.

Organizations are also "permeable": stories can be imported from surrounding social contexts. People may find that these imported stories can give them agency to change the organization, or at least how it sees itself (Ernst & Jensen Schleiter, 2021). Think, for example, how stories that illustrate and explain the devastating effects of climate change are beginning to change how some organizations use resources. However, while the social world outside the organization can provide story resources, it can also provide challenges. Stories in organizations are not always consistent or predictable in their effects because of such challenges, since as the context changes over time stories can become more or less persuasive (Parry & Kempster, 2014; Petriglieri & Petriglieri, 2015). New times and new challenges may require new stories. For example, the grand narrative of human progress and liberty seems to have gone off the rails in recent years, and we need to find new stories to make this kind of vision possible again. However, despite all of the possible changes that can occur in an organization, its external environment and the individuals within it, the challenge to show personal stability in this maelstrom remains. That is because some coherence and consistency between self-narratives and responsive actions and behaviors is always required for leader work, in order to communicate integrity (Treviño & Brown, 2004).

Individual stories and identity work

To reshape or guide an organizational narrative, leader work requires that we author a story while at the same time appearing as the narrator within it. This is a challenging task and is likely to require some work on an individual narrative, before the organizational story can be crafted. In many ways, crafting our own story is an everyday activity and is implicit in identity work (Beech, Linstead & Sims, 2007). Leader work does not require (and indeed would be undone by) the creation of some desirable but clearly fictitious story about who we are. Instead, narrative crafting ties together moments of identity work, memory and conversation into something that seems, for us, to be a coherent and realistic story about who we are (Wilson, 2004). However, the same processes are also connected to the development and maintenance of much wider stories. Thus, Ganz et al. (2023) explain the broad range of narratives, and the activities that we use to construct them, as having two important purposes, neither of which is necessarily deliberate. The first purpose is to support the construction of a particular identity, as mentioned earlier. That is, connecting micro stories together to explain purposive change, or alternatively showing appropriate consistency over time, can be integral to identity work. Using micro stories in this way builds a cumulative case or overall narrative, which supports an internal sense of self and an external impression of who we are. The second purpose is to add to the resources of our particular culture. Micro stories and more elaborate or extended forms can both communicate and preserve understandings of how we learned to deal with past problems.

If we focus on the first level in this picture, we can see that narrative is not just a chronicle of the past arranged in a logical order, but also reveals something of how we value and make sense of the world, ourselves and each other. Sparrowe (2005) explains that this is a process of "emplotment": the story helps us to integrate contingencies and choices into a meaningful whole, which provides an account of why we commit to a particular idea of who we are, and what that means for us. Reflexive practice can help us in the construction of this persuasive story of ourselves and a clear sense of who we are, as well as defending that sense of self from identity threats (Barker Caza et al., 2018; Costas & Fleming, 2009; Ellis & Ybema, 2010; Sveningsson & Alvesson, 2003). The support that story-crafting supplies for identity work is effective because narrative helps us to make sense of short-term experiences, through connecting them to a wider frame of meaning. For example, embodied and emotional reflexive practice, as discussed in earlier chapters, can be difficult to capture in words; micro stories can help preserve the insights that come to us this way (Hibbert, 2021a). Think, for example, about the story you might tell about first meeting someone who made your heart beat faster, or an incident that caused you distress. The micro story helps to capture the intensity of the experience that is signaled by embodied and emotional sensations and perceptions (Hibbert, Beech et al., 2022), and might preserve a key moment in your life story. In this way, narrative also helps us to remember and connect the transient experiences of our lives into a larger story, recognizing that our sense of who we are may change over time.[1] In addition, building on experiences of responding to identity threats over time may help us to be proactive in developing a future-oriented self-narrative (Ahuja et al., 2019; Jonason, 2019).

An awareness of how we change over time, as revealed through reflexive practice, therefore provides some key benefits in terms of self-understanding. However, this awareness of how we change also opens up some troublesome questions about the idea of being authentic in our leader work (Algera & Lips-Wiersma, 2012). Sparrowe (2005) explains that stories can help to explain how we change over time, yet remain consistent in a particular aspect of our identity, but this means that it can be difficult to connect our sense of self with a fully fixed set of values or attributes. If our identity takes a narrative form or is best explained in that way, it necessarily includes change. A simple comparison of who you were when you graduated from high school (if you can remember!) with the person you are today should make this point obvious. It is also important to remember that we each have multiple identities that are important to us. Stories provide a way of presenting ourselves coherently and consistently, despite these multiple identities that we might be attached to, in addition to the changes and challenges that we note and navigate through reflexive practice (Hibbert et al., 2019). Our stories also help us to see ourselves and how we have changed from the perspective of an interested observer, as well as helping others to contrast our narrative with their own observations to reveal other aspects of ourselves (Sparrowe, 2005; Wilson, 2004; see also Chapter 5 for a detailed discussion on this point). However, composing and sharing stories about ourselves can also feel like a risky business, and not just for us: if we are engaged in leader work, the stories we tell about ourselves may be interpreted as setting implicit norms in the organization (Fourie, 2023). Crafting and sharing our story may be both exposing and impactful, and for that reason, Ganz et al. (2023) argue that the process is laced with emotion, requires a certain degree of courage and also requires us to take responsibility for the effects that our stories may have when they are shared.

The stories we tell (ourselves and others) are open to more than just a once-and-forever interpretation, too. They provide a resource for revisiting our experiences and re-evaluating our self-understanding. Maclean et al. (2012) conducted research with senior business executives that showed how they used their own stories as a repository of experience that could be mined through thoughtful reflexive practice. The participants in their research were able to recognize useful knowledge in their retrospective engagement with their self-narratives, and use this knowledge as the basis for developing experience-informed strategies for future action. Their stories supported an emotional transformation, too: the participants, looking back on their elite business careers, constructed narratives that shifted from past difficulties to forward-looking optimistic perspectives. These benefits are to be expected since as we develop over time, our ability to interpret and reinterpret experience develops too (Hibbert et al., 2017). Re-experiencing our lives through reflecting on our own stories at a later time can help us to remember the importance and impact of partially forgotten experiences and help us to enrich the story-of-self that we share with others (Mirvis & Ayas, 2003). Overall, once we understand how our own stories communicate a picture of coherence and consistency despite (or more likely necessarily involving) inevitable change, we are in a better position to think about how we might develop the public and persuasive narratives that are intrinsic to leader work.

Public forms of narrative and leader work

One of the most established arguments for the benefits of story-telling for leaders is offered by Denning (2011), who argues that stories can be constructed in a range of ways to suit a variety of purposes: stimulating action, often through the use of a short, concise narrative based on a particular event; communicating who you are, through a rich and engaging narrative; communicating the organization's identity or brand, by supporting the sharing of micro stories by connected clients or customers; seeking to support values, through moral tales that might resemble parables; encouraging collaboration by seeding story-telling in a group; countering gossip, by creating a shareable, engaging anecdote that tackles the issue being discussed; and sharing problem-solving knowledge through stories. Shoup and Hinrichs (2021) align with Denning (2011) in the uses of narrative and in the requirements for effective story-telling in organizations: having the right style for the right kind of story, but always making individuals feel that they are the focus of the conversation about the story; regard for the truth; and careful preparation to support thoughtful and effective delivery. Denning (2011) also outlines the basic form of a story, features which apply in greater or lesser detail in the different types he outlines. In sum, these are the expected features of a beginning, middle and end but also includes the requirement for a twist in the plot, and lessons learned by characters who we perceive to be realistic. He also emphasizes how a story-teller's captivation in the story will also have the effect of engaging listeners. We are all drawn into the world of a well-told story, which can have a strong influence on us.

Others have highlighted the use of particular genres of narrative as appealing motivational tools in organizations. A good example of this motivational effect is provided in Steele and Lovelace's (2023) account of the use of underdog stories. There is a potential downside in long-term reliance on a particular genre like this: such stories may become *too* appealing, leaving the organization in a confused state if success makes the underdog story less credible over time. However, even if the story seems appealing, currently salient and well crafted, in most organizations trust in leaders and "official" narratives is not automatic. Indeed, perhaps the reverse is more likely, and "underground narratives" that challenge official stories may circulate (Bathurst & Monin, 2010). These alternative stories may be tacit, too, and Carlsen (2016) explains that unspoken stories can still have an influence through the ways that they have been taken up in people's practices and woven into organizational culture. The practices can imply a particular (kind of) story without it needing to be voiced, through constantly reconnecting with the cultural backdrop.

A background of "stories we live by", which are not explicitly shared, can make a deliberately crafted story feel wrong without it being obvious why. This can be a particular problem when the newly crafted story is trying to drive change. In addition, people may be well aware that stories can be used manipulatively in a number of ways, such as distracting criticism through an entertaining performance, tugging at our heartstrings or painting a convincing picture of an ideal but unlikely future (Auvinen, Lämsä, Sintonen & Takala, 2013). Furthermore, in family firms and others with a long heritage, there may be a backdrop of deliberately shared stories that are used to preserve memories of the founders and their actions (Hoon, Brinkmann & Baluch, 2023). In all these cases, stories about the future may struggle to resonate with the cherished narratives of the past. Even so, narratives may still be able to serve the positive purposes that Denning (2011) describes, over time. But for the desired effect to be achieved in an honest and convincing way, some more fundamental and foundational leader work is required. In part, this preliminary work is done through reflexive practice, identity work and the crafting of a personal narrative, as described in earlier chapters and in the preceding parts of this chapter. Those forms of preparatory work may be enough, or a further step may be required. This additional step involves a more collaborative construction of a "public narrative". Ganz et al. (2023), with a focus on community organizing, explain that public narrative needs to connect the collective story of the community with a leader's personal story and ground both in a clear description of the here and now. They suggest that stories combined in this way can enable groups to live out common values in the context of a shared purpose.

Ganz et al. (2023) also argue that since everyone tells stories we can all build on this, since we do it almost instinctively. Thus, developing a craft of story-telling is within everyone's reach. However, building on instinctive foundations is not necessarily straightforward and may require some formal learning, in which an individual's sense of self and story-telling capability are developed together (Armstrong & McCain, 2021). That is why I have combined those elements in this chapter. The core achievement from this combined approach is to move from a rather instinctive approach to story-telling to a more intentional approach (Ganz et al., 2023).

Up to this point, we can be forgiven for thinking that stories only support a kind of "top-down" approach to leader work, but Orr and Bennett (2016, following Fairhurst & Uhl-Bien, 2012) give a rich account of a relational approach to leadership, and how that connects with the processes of story-telling. In their work focused on public-sector leadership, they give an account of how stories provide a way for members of an organization to engage with and understand a leader's goals (Sternberg, 2008), perhaps reshaping those goals through their interpretive engagement as they do so. Similarly, Stark, Reif and Schiebler (2022) underline the importance of considering what the members of the organization might need from stories, including how much or little personal material about the leader/story-teller they might find appropriate, as well as being alert to the fact that multiple interpretations of any story are likely.

Dealing with multiple interpretations, some of which may be at odds with the intentions of the story crafter, requires processes that provide feedback (Stark et al., 2022). Orr and Bennett (2016) identified three kinds of storying processes that support a relational approach, incorporating feedback, which could also be applied to contexts quite different from the public service setting of their study. The first process is *inviting an emotional connection* through recasting the organization in a different way: in this process, a common emotional response brings different and diverse groups together. Similarly, Gans and Zhan (2023) argue that the most persuasive approach to supporting employee participation is through constructing and sharing stories that show the possibility of future benefits for the individual *and* organization.

The second process outlined by Orr and Bennett (2016) is focused on *making sense of organizational realities* through bringing people together into the process of interpreting the story, allowing for and engaging with competing narratives as part of the process. This process helps incorporate a wider understanding of change, includes differing expectations and connects a potential for action into the story. Thus, stories can guide sense-making, point towards possible solutions to problems and help to define who is an insider or outsider, in relation to the specific groups and projects that bring potential action to life (Havermans, Keegan & Den Hartog, 2015).

The third of Orr and Bennett's (2016) processes is *provoking reflection on practices and assumptions*. This process is more leader-driven and seeks to challenge and disrupt understandings and practices, although it is mobilized in the expectation that there will be considerable skepticism and resistance about the potential and desirability of change, or perhaps tensons between alternative possibilities (Maclean, Harvey, Golant & Sillince, 2021).

Overall, while their processes do help to demonstrate a narrative approach that is not purely leader-driven, Orr and Bennett (2016) note that it was a struggle to maintain a sense of collective engagement and leadership while at the same time enabling individual action and choice where necessary. They point to the tension between neutralizing individual agency on the one hand or, on the other hand, collapsing the collective dimension by falling into the trap of charismatic or heroic models of leadership.

One way to avoid slipping into heroic models of leadership is to balance "writing" a story for the organization with "reading" the different stories that others in the organization can tell, an exchange which can lead to changes in the leader self-narrative and in the collective story. This balancing form of leader work is best achieved through reflexive dialogue with others, which may perhaps include people from beyond the organization (Hibbert et al., 2016). That is, such dialogue can help to keep stories open to new ideas from within and beyond the present context (Fischer-Appelt & Dernbach, 2023). Through maintaining this openness, reflexive dialogue can thus help an individual to continue to grow and develop in their potential for leader work, and lead to new plot lines for stories that engage others in a shared future.

Reflexive dialogue: balancing "writing" with "reading"

Reflexive dialogue that keeps us open to change, and helps to update the self-narratives we author and the collective narratives we orchestrate through leader work, builds on relationally reflexive practice, as discussed in Chapter 5. However, with story crafting in mind, there are three approaches to dialogue that reconnect with and further develop key points from that earlier discussion. These approaches are dialogue with ourselves, through working with written accounts of our experiences, dialogue with texts written by others that help us to see things differently (such as novels, that can help us develop empathetic understanding: Mar, 2018; Mar et al., 2021; Rain & Mar, 2021) or through conversation. All these approaches provide the opportunity for learning in a relational context, which resonates with the nature of leader work. Indeed, Stead and Elliott (2012) see reflexive dialogue as pivotal to understanding how leadership learning mobilizes, interprets and builds on experience in a relational process.

Dialogue with the self seems like a paradoxical idea, but having a written account to revisit makes this possible. As we change over time, our perspective on the self-narrative that we authored at an earlier point is also changed. We interpret things differently as we and our circumstances change (Hibbert et al., 2016). Thus, while reading our own stories might reawaken our feelings about particular experiences (Mirvis & Ayas, 2003), it can also leave us feeling struck (Cunliffe, 2002) by differences in how we would understand or act in similar situations today.

The process of re-engaging with our own self-narratives can also help us to reassemble these stories, using new interpretations to reveal unexpected insights – perhaps when we come across some new "key" to interpretation at a particular point. For example, in my own personal narrative I needed to try to reconcile how experience working in industry, management consultancy and academia joins up, along with my involvement in a range of voluntary roles. I also needed to think about how formal study at different times in subjects as varied as chemistry, theology and management (not to mention short courses in languages and a truly disastrous exploration of expressionist theatre), and interests in fiction and poetry, made any kind of sense. What does all that do for leader work? It might provide the material for an interesting story on one level, but it does not look like a conventional route to holding senior management positions in academia, as I have done. Yet, I seem to have been successful in the leader work required in such roles. The integrating clue comes in the need for creativity. Leader work involves crafting stories, which is a creative process, and Epstein (2020) has collated evidence from a range of research studies that establish that creativity comes from a breadth of interests and experiences. In addition, since leader work is most relevant and necessary in times of uncertainty (Ganz, 2010) when the future direction is unclear, the breadth of understanding that comes from a wide range of interests may be doubly important: it provides different ways of seeing patterns and possibilities that a highly trained but narrow specialist view might miss.

Realizing and valuing the surprising breadth of your own story can also help you to be open to the value of the wide range of interests and insights that others may have, and to value reflexive dialogue in which both conversation partners can learn and change from all the other has to offer (Hibbert et al., 2016). However, difficulties can arise if a reflexive dialogue simply becomes discussion at one extreme (where there is only one "right" answer to be identified) or at the other extreme, lacks critical engagement by just accepting everything at face value without exploring the depth behind an insight. That is, if the dialogue never touches on the hinterland of our conversation partner's rich story, we might not recognize the significance of their insights. For example, Larsson and Knudsen (2022) describe how participants in a leadership development program based on peer discussion were able to share experience from isolated cases and their individual interpretations, to enrich a shared repertoire. However, they also point out that the climate of the discussions, in which each participant treated the other respectfully as an expert on their own leadership practice, prevented participants from reaching a deeper level of constructive critical questioning. They also found that it was difficult for external facilitators to disrupt these constraints to make a helpful process of critical questioning possible, even when invited to do so. The upshot is that to avoid win–lose discussions or uncritical engagement, participants in a reflexive dialogue need to establish how to enable and maintain the right level of challenge and depth of inquiry for themselves. For example, Paton, Chia and Burt (2014) helped their executive clients to explore, in a reflexive dialogue process, plausible alternative futures in ways that helped to unsettle taken-for-granted assumptions. This was effective because the imaginative possibilities and problems in fictional (but plausible) futures took the executives beyond their immediate domain of professional expertise, which could no longer be relied on. They were encouraged and enabled to engage with each other in depth, in imagined future situations where protecting professional pride became irrelevant.

While Paton et al.'s (2014) approach was non-threatening, in most circumstances of dialogue some capacity for coping with challenge is needed. This capacity is necessary even if the challenges that come are implicit rather than explicit. This is because, if you are truly learning in dialogue, new insights may open up in ways that question your current assumptions. Thus, Dyer and Hurd (2016) show that when deeply held beliefs are challenged the reflexive learning process is fraught with difficult emotion, and is generally messy, rather than linear. This means getting dialogue to work may require a capacity for reflexive practice which includes embodiment and emotions as well as thoughts, which is why so much attention was paid to the foundations of reflexive practice in Chapters 2 to 5. The capacity for reflexive practice can also help with the management of any conflict that may arise, through supporting a better understanding of our own motivations and the influence of the context on those motivations (Rothman, 2014), enabling a more empathetic approach. For example, Long, Linabary, Buzzanell, Mouton and Rao (2020) describe how co-learning partnerships, built on an ethic of care, could support challenging forms of dialogue that lead to reflexive formation of the "whole person". In their case, this was because there was a willingness for the dialogue to include disagreement without trying to resolve it, along with a recognition that people's individual lived experiences were important and valid sources of knowledge.

Overall, using reflexive dialogue effectively requires attention to a number of constraints and conditions, in order to overcome the problems and challenges that can otherwise get in the way. Building on a range of insights (for example, Hibbert et al., 2017; Larsson & Knudsen, 2022; Long et al., 2020), I summarize the necessary conditions for helpful reflexive dialogue in this way:

Involving others: While dialogue can be used as a model for introspection, even in that case the use of literature and art works as "conversation partners" is helpful, rather than relying purely on your own thoughts. You need someone or something that can "contest" your opinions and assumptions, and help you to see things differently. Examples of this kind of art for me include Pablo Picasso's *Guernica*, Ursula Le Guin's novel *The Left Hand of Darkness* and Mahmoud Darwish's poetic autobiography *In the Presence of Absence*. I need to emphasize that the point is not to adopt the worldview offered by a work of art, but to recognize that it challenges you and explore why that might be so. Just like a "real" conversation partner, a great work of art can interrupt our comfortable ways of thinking so that we can examine them.

Maintaining humility: It is a central tenet of dialogue that there is always something to learn from others, and for that reason we are all mutually dependent when it comes to reflexive practice and the understandings it can provide.

Building a caring context: Processes of reflexive dialogue can be challenging and, especially if the aims include supporting ethical development, there is a need to establish a community or context where mutual care is normalized.

Maintaining an open mind: A truly open process of dialogue needs to include the recognition that an initial spark of insight may just be a moment in a process that leads to something deeper, if we keep our curiosity and criticality alive. This is because the flow of dialogue is not predictable, and it is a mistake to reach a conclusion too soon.

Recognizing uncertainties and tacit understandings: Building on the principle of an open mind, we need to recognize that there are always residual uncertainties. This means that dialogue is part of a process that develops cumulative experience in ways that might support intuition and bricolage, rather than explicit knowledge.

With the conditions in place, we can be more focused on what is going on in reflexive dialogue. It will include two modes of engagement and interpretation (Hibbert et al., 2016). The first and most superficial mode is instrumental exchange, in which the partners in dialogue are simply seeking to find a missing "jigsaw piece" of knowledge to address their current problem(s). The second mode is more open and developmental and involves curiosity-driven dialogue, with the intention to explore what we might find out from and about each other, without needing to have an immediate purpose for the knowledge that emerges. There will be a place for both modes, but in order to keep the stories about ourselves and the organization open to change, the second – curiosity-driven dialogue – is the most important. In addition, for those involved with leader work, engagement with this mode of dialogue means that the stories you construct for the organization can continue to reflect and resonate with others, through a better understanding of who they are and how they are changing.

Curiosity-driven dialogue also has the benefit of providing another way of developing breadth and flexibility, so that someone who is involved with leader work is open to multiple possibilities and views each time they face a new challenge (Hibbert et al., 2016; Raelin, 2007). It is one of the paradoxes of leader work that decisive action, and the development of a clear sense of direction that guides others, is needed most when the situation is flooded with uncertainty. Dialogue in our formation, long before a tricky situation is upon us, is likely to help us to have a range of intuitive options in such crises. When the situation is not a time-sensitive crisis, dialogue with others can help us explore the situation from different perspectives, too. Leader work involves navigating uncertainty, but that does not mean that there can only be one navigator.

In conclusion, reflexive dialogue helps us to prevent the story of ourselves and our organizations from becoming fixed and closed, and it supports leader work that is based on the development of the individual and the organization together. Our stories tell us who we are and give us enough confidence to act in uncertain times. Our reflexive practice, especially in dialogue, helps to keep our humility in place to prevent us from developing a dangerous overconfidence about how the story ends, or what we need to do get there. We always need to be ready for a twist in the plot.

A last word on leader work

A return to the foundations

In the opening chapter of this book, I offered a definition of leader work that may have seemed, on some levels, to be counterintuitive.

Leader work combines inward and outward forms of work. The inward work involves: developing our knowledge of ourselves, our capabilities and our limitations through self-examination and connecting with others; building up our capacity for judgment; and gaining confidence in using intuition and imagination thoughtfully in situations of complexity and uncertainty. The outward work involves learning to express a leader identity that is both true to ourselves and recognized by relevant groups and organizations, so that we are trusted to help them navigate and narrate a path through uncertainty.

My hope is that having arrived at this point the definition rings true for you, although it is likely that some questions will remain. There are two questions that I have anticipated at this point. The first is: how do you develop your ability to "narrate a path through uncertainty"? While I have touched on the structure and conditions for crafting an effective story (Denning, 2011; Shoup & Hinrichs, 2021), that is not going to enable you to write one just by reading about those requirements. Instead, it is necessary to work through the "inward" forms of work first, while bearing in mind that reflexive practice is an ongoing commitment and not something that you complete once and for all. However, with sufficient experience of reflexive practice you can then approach the "outward" forms of work when you are ready, focusing on your own identity and self-narrative before thinking about crafting narratives for others as the final integrative step.

The second question that arises is: do you have to wait to be "fully formed" before taking on leader work? The answer to that is no, for two reasons: first, our formation is never completed; and second, the world won't wait. While leader work may reach its ultimate expression in the ability to craft persuasive narratives that guide an organization through uncertainty, a good deal of work needs to take place in everyday contexts and on smaller scales. That is why the *direct* relevance of reflexive practice and identity work, for leader work, has been spelled out in Chapters 2 to 6, and suggested actions for applying these insights are provided at the end of each chapter. In addition, while there is no shortcut to growth and development, I recognize that the emergent situations for leader work may also require some quick-fixes. For that reason, a brief outline of some leadership tactics, based on the work of Fourie (2023), is included here. After that outline I also offer some "reflexive heuristics" to provide a check against overreliance on tactics and keep the possibility of reflexive practice alive day to day.

Short-term tactics

Fourie (2023)[2] reviewed and compiled a useful list of leadership tactics studied in earlier research, which have been shown to have an effect on influencing others to support organizational goals or initiatives. He lists two kinds of tactics, "soft" and "hard", and summarizes the effectiveness (or otherwise) of these tools. From my perspective, the preferred "soft tactics" are largely concerned with motivating others through the familiar tools of Aristotelian rhetoric (Hühn & Meyer, 2023). Thus, I interpret these tactics in this way:

Logos (an appeal based on rational argument): Leader work can (and perhaps always should) involve the use of facts and evidence to persuade others to engage in a course of action to support shared goals. Fourie (2023) indicates that this could involve the development of an inclusive approach that allows others to contribute facts and evidence too, but also signals that such an approach needs to be an accepted norm within an organization for it to be effective. A variation on this approach is to articulate the personal benefits an individual can expect if they engage with the planned course of action.

Pathos (an appeal based on the audience's emotions): Emotional appeals may either be based on concern for stakeholders or beneficiaries of the organization's work or be based on established relationships between those undertaking leader work and others. Largely, this kind of motivation relies on care for particular individuals or communities, and the benefits that can be obtained for them (or mitigating the risk of disadvantage or difficulty that they face). However, one variation is to appeal to the individual's regard for themselves, rather than their regard for others, through ingratiation. If you have ever been praised to the skies as "the only person who can handle the task", you will know how this feels.

Ethos (an appeal based on values): Values can be motivating when an inspirational narrative that resonates with organization members is crafted, and/or when organization members are involved through consultation or collaboration in setting the desired direction. However, it is best not to use consultation or collaboration if you do not intend to honor the process: when such processes are pseudo-democratic window dressing, they can be seriously demotivating. That is because it establishes duplicity as an organizational value, which is a corrosive outcome.

The "hard" tactics that Fourie (2023) mentions are largely to do with the mobilization of management power and formal authority, rather than leader work. They include offering rewards in exchange for compliance, using formal authority in explicit ways (which may be effective and expected in very hierarchical organizations, such as the police or military) and the use of borrowed authority from a coalition of powerful individuals.

Fourie (2023) found that all of the tactics could be effective in certain contexts and situations, whereas the use of direct pressure (including threats) was not. In addition to Fourie's insights about the effects of the different tactics, I suggest that there is an additional concern in relation to using pressure. Reflexive practice should help you to be aware of your emotions and your emotional impact on others. So, something may be slipping in your practice if you find yourself using pressure, or you may be experiencing unacknowledged stress that is influencing your behavior. In addition, a real risk in highly stressful environments is that pressure tactics can become normalized. In such cases crafting stories and shifting approaches to disrupt that normalization are part of the leader work agenda, rather than allowing it to continue. Moreover, stories can include and tie together multiple "soft" tactics by appealing to logic, emotions and values within the same narrative. However, in crisis situations story crafting can feel out of reach, so I offer some reflexive heuristics (rules of thumb), as a way of keeping reflexive practice in mind when you are in tactical mode.

Reflexive heuristics

It is always risky to offer some summary points that cannot hope to fully integrate complex sets of insights. But I hope that the points below will be useful reminders that help to connect with the richer ideas about reflexive practice for leader work explained throughout the book. These summary points are the brief advice I give to anyone taking on a new role that involves leader work (but only if they ask me to offer advice).

Take care of your body (and mind): I hope that it should take no effort to convince you to look after your physical and mental health. But it is important to emphasize that unless you pay regular attention to your body and mind, especially if your work life is intense, you may notice problems when it is too late. Embodied reflexive practice may help you to pay attention to what is going on within you and around you, but if you notice problems seek professional advice.

Be ready to recalibrate your sense of alarm: It is normal to have a strong emotional reaction when encountering an unexpected and perhaps overwhelming challenge. But try to see if your emotions are asking you to pay attention rather than seek safety! Emotional reflexive practice will help you spot that your feelings are highlighting something new you need to understand, most of the time, rather than something to fear. In addition, many things that seem alarming in the first few months of a new role can often feel routine once you have settled in.

Learn how to apologize gracefully, and mean it: Attention to thoughtful reflexive practice will help you realize that you sometimes need to rely on intuition, imagination and bricolage. Everyone does. This means that we will all get things wrong sometimes, especially when challenges are complex and unfamiliar. Admitting that you were wrong is a dignified thing to do, and that includes apologizing to anyone who may have been affected by your error even if it was a well-intentioned mistake.

Make sure you have friends with different experiences and views: find people who don't always agree with you to be part of your network, preferably people you think are smart and who do not work for the same organization as you. The goal here is to provide a balance of constructive, critical inquiry and compassionate support for each other: you will be in no place to take advice when you have been broken by an experience, and neither will they. Caring friends will recognize how you are – or will ask – before speaking. The benefits of relational reflexive practice in these kinds of relationships will accrue on both sides.

Conclusion

Using short-term leadership tactics needs to be undertaken thoughtfully, with regard for what it might mean for the believability of your self-narrative and the organization's motivating story. Choose wisely. I also encourage you to think about the reflexive heuristics offered above, so that you do not become over-reliant on a limited toolbox of tactics.

In the interest of balancing short-term and long-term resources, I suggest you engage with novels and biographies that could help as "conversation partners" in your longer-term reflexive practice. The point here is not to find books that directly address leadership, but instead to seek out texts that help you to see things differently, or help you to understand the lives of others in ways that question your assumptions. My starter suggestions for books of these kinds are two that I have cited earlier, Ursula Le Guin's *The Left Hand of Darkness* and Mahmoud Darwish's *In the Presence of Absence*, but I have no wish to dictate your taste – choose books that appeal to you, as long as they do not simply reinforce your settled views. In any case I hope that you will find some time for reading as part of the continuing journey of self-development for leader work, which always involves unexpected stories. To conclude: as you prepare for new surprises and new questions, I wish you the best of luck.

Notes

1 It may be helpful, with that in mind, to keep an occasional diary, noting the micro stories that seem significant to you. Story-telling performers, like Dicks (2018), also suggest a range of alternative ways of capturing "story-worthy" incidents.

2 See especially pp74–78 of his book.

REFERENCES

Adjepong, A. 2019. Invading ethnography: A queer of color reflexive practice. *Ethnography*, 20: 27–46.

Ahmadi, A. & Vogel, B. 2023. Knowing but not enacting leadership: Navigating the leadership knowing-doing gap in leveraging leadership development. *Academy of Management Learning & Education*, 22(3): 507–530.

Ahuja, S. 2023. Professional identity threats in interprofessional collaborations: A case of architects in professional service firms. *Journal of Management Studies*, 60: 428–453.

Ahuja, S., Heizmann, H. & Clegg, S. 2019. Emotions and identity work: Emotions as discursive resources in the constitution of junior professionals' identities. *Human Relations*, 72: 988–1009.

Ajjawi, R., Hilder, J., Noble, C., Teodorczuk, A. & Billett, S. 2020. Using video-reflexive ethnography to understand complexity and change practice. *Medical Education*, doi: 10.1111/medu.14156.

Alam, M. & Singh, P. 2021. Performance feedback interviews as affective events: An exploration of the impact of emotion regulation of negative performance feedback on supervisor–employee dyads. *Human Resource Management Review*, 31: 100740.

Algera, M. & Lips-Wiersma, M. 2012. Radical authentic leadership: Co-creating the conditions under which all members of the organization can be authentic. *Leadership Quarterly*, 23(1): 118–131.

Allen, M. & Tsakiris, M. 2019. The body as first prior: Interoceptive predictive processing and the primacy of self-models. In: Tsakiris, M. & De Preester, H. (eds), *The Interoceptive Mind*, pp27–45. Oxford: Oxford University Press.

Allen, S. 2017. Learning from Friends: Developing appreciations for unknowing in reflexive practice. *Management Learning*, 48(2): 125–139.

Alvesson, M. & Sveningsson, S. 2003. Good visions, bad micro-management and ugly ambiguity: Contradictions of (non)leadership in a knowledge-intensive organization. *Organization Studies*, 24(6): 961–988.

Alvesson, M. & Willmott, H. 2002. Identity regulation as organizational control: Producing the appropriate individual. *Journal of Management Studies*, 39(5): 619–644.

Amiot, C.E., de la Sablonniere, R., Terry, D.J. & Smith, J.R. 2007. Integration of social identities in the self: Toward a cognitive-developmental model. *Personality and Social Psychology Review*, 11: 364–388.

Aquino, K. & Reed, A. 2002. The self-importance of moral identity. *Journal of Personality and Social Psychology*, 83(6): 1423–1440.

Archer, M. 2007. *Making Our Way through the World*. Cambridge: Cambridge University Press.

Armstrong, J. & McCain, K. 2021. Narrative pedagogy for leadership education: Stories of leadership efficacy, self-identity, and leadership development. *Journal of Leadership Studies*, 14(4): 60–70.

Aronowitz, R., Deener, A., Keene, D., Schnittker, J. & Tach, L. 2015. Cultural reflexivity in health research and practice. *American Journal of Public Health*, 105(S3): S403–S408.

Ashkanasy, N., Humphrey, R. & Huy, Q. 2017. Integrating emotions and affect in theories of management. *Academy of Management Review*, 42: 175–189.

Auvinen, T., Lämsä, A., Sintonen, T. & Takala T. 2013. Leadership manipulation and ethics in storytelling. *Journal of Business Ethics*, 116: 415–431.

Babo-Rebelo, M. & Tallon-Baudry, C. 2019. Interoceptive signals, brain dynamics and subjectivity. In: Tsakiris, M. & De Preester, H. (eds), *The Interoceptive Mind*, pp46–62. Oxford: Oxford University Press.

Baker, T. & Nelson, R.E. 2005. Creating something from nothing: Resource construction through entrepreneurial bricolage. *Administrative Science Quarterly*, 50(3): 329–366.

Barker Caza B., Moss S. & Vough H. 2018. From synchronizing to harmonizing: The process of authenticating multiple work identities. *Administrative Science Quarterly*, 63(4): 703–745.

Bataille, C. & Vough, H. 2022. More than the sum of my parts: An intrapersonal network approach to identity work in response to identity opportunities and threats. *Academy of Management Review*, 47(1): 93–115.

Bathurst, R. & Monin, N. 2010. Finding myth and motive in language: A narrative of organizational change. *Journal of Management Inquiry*, 19(3): 262–272.

Beech, N. 2011. Liminality and the practices of identity reconstruction. *Human Relations*, 64(2): 285–302.

Beech, N. 2017. Identity at work: An enquiry-based approach to therapeutically inspired management. *International Journal of Management Reviews*, 19(3): 357–370.

Beech, N., Gilmore, C., Hibbert, P. & Ybema, S. 2016. Identity-in-the-work and musicians' struggles: The production of self-questioning identity work. *Work, Employment and Society*, 30(3): 506–522.

Beech, N., Linstead, A. & Sims, D. (eds). 2007. *Researching Identity: Concepts and Methods*. London: Routledge.

Beets, K. & Goodman, S. 2012. Evaluating a training programme for executive coaches. *Journal of Human Resource Management*, 10: 425–435.

Benjamin, B. & O'Reilly, C. 2011. Becoming a leader: Early career challenges faced by MBA graduates. *Academy of Management Learning & Education*, 10: 452–472.

Bernhard, F. & Labaki, R. 2021. Moral emotions in family businesses: Exploring vicarious guilt of the next generation. *Family Business Review*, 34(2): 193–212.

Berntson, G., Gianaros, P. & Tsakiris, M. 2019. Interoception and the autonomic nervous system: Bottom up meets top-down. In: Tsakiris, M. & De Preester, H. (eds), *The Interoceptive Mind*, pp3–23. Oxford: Oxford University Press.

Berti, M., Jarvis, W., Nikolova, N. & Pitsis, A. 2021. Embodied phronetic pedagogy: Cultivating ethical and moral capabilities in postgraduate business students. *Academy of Management Learning & Education*, 20: 6–29.

Bigo, V. & Islam, G. 2022. Embodiment and management learning: Understanding the role of bodily analogy in a yoga-based learning model. *Academy of Management Learning & Education*, 21(4): 648–668.

Bissett, N. & Saunders, S. 2015. Criticality and collegiality: A method for humanizing everyday practice? *Journal of Management Education*, 39: 597–625.

Bohm, D. 2004. *On Dialogue*. London: Routledge.

Borins, S. 2012. Making narrative count: A narratological approach to public management innovation. *Journal of Public Administration Research and Theory*, 22: 165–189.

Boudens, C. 2005. The story of work: A narrative analysis of workplace emotion. *Organization Studies*, 26(9): 1285–1306.

Brown, A. 2015. Identities and identity work in organizations. *International Journal of Management Reviews*, 17(1): 20–40.

Brown, A. 2017. Identity work and organizational identification. *International Journal of Management Reviews*, 19(3): 296–317.

Brown, A. & Coupland, C. 2015. Identity threats, identity work and elite professionals. *Organization Studies*, 36(10): 1315–1336.

Brown, P. 2022. *On Vulnerability*. London: Routledge.

Brown, P. & de Graaf, S. 2013. Considering a future which may not exist: The construction of time and expectations amidst advanced-stage cancer. *Health, Risk & Society*, 15: 543–560.

Burkitt, I. 2012. Emotional reflexivity: Feeling, emotion and imagination in reflexive dialogues. *Sociology*, 46: 458–472.

Bush, J., Welsh, D., Baer, M. & Waldman, D. 2021. Discouraging unethicality versus encouraging ethicality: Unraveling the differential effects of prevention- and promotion-focused ethical leadership. *Personnel Psychology*, 74: 29–54.

Caetano, A. 2017. Coping with life: A typology of personal reflexivity. *The Sociological Quarterly*, 58: 32–50.

Cain, C., Frazer, M. & Kilaberia, T. 2019. Identity work within attempts to transform healthcare: Invisible team processes. *Human Relations*, 72(2): 370–396.

Callagher, L., Elsahn, Z., Hibbert, P., Korber, S. & Siedlok, F. 2021. Early career researchers' identity threats in the field: The shelter and shadow of collective support. *Management Learning*, 52(4): 442–465.

Carlsen, A. 2016. On the tacit side of organizational identity: Narrative unconscious and figured practice. *Culture and Organization*, 22(2): 107–135.

Carollo, L. & Guerci, M. 2018. "Activists in a suit": Paradoxes and metaphors in sustainability managers' identity work. *Journal of Business Ethics*, 148(2): 249–268.

Carroll, B. 2016. Leadership as identity: A practice-based exploration. In J.A. Raelin (ed.), *Leadership as Practice*, pp91–109. London: Routledge.

Carstenson, M., Sørenson, E. & Torfing, J. 2022. Why we need bricoleurs to foster robust governance solutions in turbulent times. *Public Administration*, 101: 36–52.

Casey, A.J. & Goldman, E.F. 2010. Enhancing the ability to think strategically: A learning model. *Management Learning*, 41: 167–185.

Cha, S. & Edmonson, A. 2006. When values backfire: Leadership, attribution, and disenchantment in a values-driven organization. *Leadership Quarterly*, 17: 57–78.

Chilvers, J. & Kearnes, M. 2020. Remaking participation in science and democracy. *Science, Technology, & Human Values*, 45: 347–380.

Ciulla, J. 2008. Leadership studies and "the fusion of horizons". *Leadership Quarterly*, 19: 393–395.

Collien, I. 2018. Critical–reflexive–political: Dismantling the reproduction of dominance in organisational learning processes. *Management Learning*, 49: 131–149.

Conroy, S. & O'Leary-Kelly, A. 2014. Letting go and moving on: Work-related identity loss and recovery. *Academy of Management Review*, 39(1): 67–87.

Conway, A.M., Tugade, M.M., Catalino, L.I. & Fredrickson, B.L. 2013. The broaden-and-build theory of positive emotions: Form, function and mechanisms. In: Boniwell, I., David, S.A. & Conley Ayers, A. (eds), *Oxford Handbook of Happiness*, pp17–34. Oxford: Oxford University Press.

Corbett-Etchevers, I. & Parmentier-Cajaiba, A. 2022. Making strategy out of everyday tools: A collective bricolage perspective. *M@n@gement*, 25(3): 39–56.

Corlett, S. 2013. Participant learning in and through research as reflexive dialogue: Being "struck" and the effects of recall. *Management Learning*, 44: 453–469.

Corlett, S., Mavin, S. & Beech, N. 2019. Reconceptualizing vulnerability and its value for managerial identity and learning. *Management Learning*, 50: 556–575.

Costas, J. & Fleming, P. 2009. Beyond dis-identification: A discursive approach to self-alienation in contemporary organizations. *Human Relations*, 62(3): 353–378.

Critchley, H. & Harrison, N. 2013. Visceral influences on brain and behavior. *Neuron*, 77: 624–638.

Cunliffe, A. 2002. Reflexive dialogical practice in management learning. *Management Learning*, 33(1): 35–61.

Cunliffe, A. 2003. Reflexive inquiry in organizational research: Questions and possibilities. *Human Relations*, 56: 983–1003.

Cunliffe, A. 2004. On becoming a critically reflexive practitioner. *Journal of Management Education*, 28: 407–426.

Cunliffe, A. 2009. The philosopher leader: On relationalism, ethics and reflexivity – a critical perspective in teaching leadership. *Management Learning*, 40: 87–101.

Cunliffe, A. 2018. Wayfaring: A scholarship of possibilities or let's not get drunk on abstraction. *M@n@gement*, 21(4): 1429–1439.

Cunliffe, A. & Hibbert, P. 2016. The philosophical basis of leadership-as-practice from a hermeneutical perspective. In: Raelin, J. (ed.), *Leadership as Practice*, pp50–69. London: Routledge.

Curtis, G. & Cerni, T. 2015. For leaders to be transformational they must think imaginatively. *Journal of Leadership Studies*, 9(3): 45–47.

Curtis, G., King, G. & Russ, A. 2017. Reexamining the relationship between thinking styles and transformational leadership: What is the contribution of imagination and emotionality? *Journal of Leadership Studies*, 11(2): 8–21.

Dailey, S. & Browning, L. 2014. Retelling stories in organizations: Understanding the functions of narrative repetition. *Academy of Management Review*, 39: 22–24.

Darwish, M. 2011. *In the Presence of Absence*. New York: Archipelago.

Dasborough, M., Ashkanasy, N., Tee, E. & Tse, H. 2009. What goes around comes around: How meso-level negative emotional contagion can ultimately determine organizational attitudes toward leaders. *Leadership Quarterly*, 20: 571–585.

Dasborough, M., Hannah, S. & Zhu, W. 2020. The generation and function of moral emotions in teams: An integrative review. *Journal of Applied Psychology*, 105(5): 433–452.

Davey, N. 2006. *Unquiet Understanding*. Albany, NY: State University of New York Press.

Day, D., Harrison, M. & Halpin, S. 2009. *An Integrative Approach to Leader Development: Connecting Adult Development, Identity, and Expertise*. New York: Psychology Press.

Denning, S. 2011. *The Leader's Guide to Storytelling: Mastering the Art and Discipline of Business Narrative*. San Francisco, CA: Jossey Bass.

Derrida, J. 1976. *Of Grammatology* (G.C. Spivak, trans.). Baltimore, MD: Johns Hopkins University Press.

Derrida, J. 1978. *Writing and Difference*. Chicago, IL: University of Chicago Press.

DeRue, D. & Ashford, S. 2010. Who will lead and who will follow? A social process of leadership identity construction in organizations. *Academy of Management Review*, 35(4): 627–647.

DeRue, D., Ashford, S. & Cotton, N. 2009. Assuming the mantle: Unpacking the process by which individuals internalize a leader identity. In L.M. Roberts & J.E. Dutton (eds), *Exploring Positive Identities and Organizations: Building a Theoretical and Research Foundation*, pp217–236. New York: Routledge.

Dicks, M. 2018. *Storyworthy*. Novato: New World Library.

Driver, M. 2013. The lack of power or the power of lack in leadership as a discursively constructed identity. *Organization Studies*, 34(3): 407–422.

Driver, M. 2015. How trust functions in the context of identity work. *Human Relations*, 68(6): 899–923.

Duarte, F. 2009. Rekindling the sociological imagination as a pedagogical package in management education. *Journal of Management Education*, 33, 59–76.

Dumont, M., Yzerbyt, V.Y., Wigboldus, D. & Gordijn, E.H. 2003. Social categorization and fear reactions to the September 11th terrorist attacks. *Personality and Social Psychology Bulletin*, 29: 1509–1520.

Dutton, D.G. & Aron, A.P. 1974. Some evidence for heightened sexual attraction under conditions of high anxiety. *Journal of Personality and Social Psychology*, 30: 510–517.

Dyer, S. & Hurd, F. 2016. "What's going on?" Developing reflexivity in the management classroom: From surface to deep learning and everything in between. *Academy of Management Learning & Education*, 15(2): 287–303.

Elbanna, S. 2015. Intuition in project management and missing links: Analyzing the predicating effects of environment and the mediating role of reflexivity. *International Journal of Project Management*, 33: 1236–1248.

Ellemers, N. 2018. Morality and social identity. In: van Zomeren, M. & Dovidio, J.F. (eds), *The Oxford Handbook of the Human Essence*, pp147–158. Oxford: Oxford University Press.

Ellis, N. & Ybema, S. 2010. Marketing identities: Shifting circles of identification in inter-organizational relationships. *Organization Studies*, 31(3): 279–305.

Empson, L., Langley, A. & Sergi, V. 2023. When everyone and no one is a leader: Constructing individual leadership identities while sustaining an organizational narrative of collective leadership. *Organization Studies*, 44(2): 201–227.

Epstein, D. 2020. *Range: How Generalists Triumph in a Specialized World*. London: Pan Books.

Ernst, J. & Jensen Schleiter, A. 2021. Organizational identity struggles and reconstruction during organizational change: Narratives as symbolic, emotional and practical glue. *Organization Studies*, 42(6): 891–910.

Evans, R., Ribbens McCarthy, J., Bowlby, S., Wouangoa, J. & Kébé, F. 2017. Producing emotionally sensed knowledge? Reflexivity and emotions in researching responses to death. *International Journal of Social Research Methodology*, 20: 585–598.

Fairhurst, G. & Uhl-Bien, M. 2012. Organizational discourse analysis (ODA): Examining leadership as a relational process. *Leadership Quarterly*, 23(6): 1043–1062.

Feldman, M., Skoldberg, K., Brown, R. & Horner, D. 2004. Making sense of stories: A rhetorical approach to narrative analysis. *Journal of Public Administration Research and Theory*, 14(2): 147–170.

Fernando, M., Reveley, J. & Learmonth, M. 2020. Identity work by a non-white immigrant business scholar: Autoethnographic vignettes of covering and accenting. *Human Relations*, 73(6): 765–788.

Fineman, S. 2006. On being positive: Concerns and counterpoints. *Academy of Management Review*, 31(2): 270–291.

Fischer, A. & Manstead, A. 2016. Social functions of emotion and emotion regulation. In: Lewis, M., Haviland-Jones, J. & Barrett, L. (eds), *Handbook of Emotions*, 4th edition, pp424–439. New York: Guilford.

Fischer-Appelt, B. & Dernbach, R. 2023. Exploring narrative strategy: The role of narratives in the strategic positioning of organizational change. *Innovation: European Journal of Social Science Research*, 36(1): 85–95.

Fotopolou, A. & Tsakiris, M. 2017. Mentalizing homeostasis: The social origins of interoceptive inference. *Neuropsychoanalysis*, 19: 3–28.

Fourie, W. 2023. *Why Leaders Fail*. London: Routledge.

Frost, P. & Robinson, S. 1999. The toxic handler: Organizational hero – and casualty. *Harvard Business Review*, 77(4): 96–106.

Gabriel, Y. 2018. Interpretation, reflexivity and imagination in qualitative research. In: Ciesielska, M. & Jemielniak, D. (eds), *Qualitative Methodologies in Organization Studies, Volume I: Theories and New Approaches*, pp137–157. London: Palgrave Macmillan.

Gadamer, H.-G. 1998. *Truth and Method*, 2nd edition. New York: Continuum.

Gallagher, S. 2000. Philosophical conceptions of the self: Implications for cognitive science. *Trends in Cognitive Science*, 4: 14–21.

Gans, R. & Zhan, M. 2023. A story about speaking up: Mediation effects of narrative persuasion on organizational voice intentions. *International Journal of Business Communication*, 60(3): 865–891.

Ganz, M. 2010. Leading change: Leadership, organization and social movements. In: Nohria, N. & Khurana, R. (eds), *Handbook of Leadership Theory and Practice*, pp527–568. Cambridge, MA: Harvard University Press.

Ganz, M., Lee Cunningham, J., Ben Ezer, I. & Segura, A. 2023. Crafting public narrative to enable collective action: A pedagogy for leadership development. *Academy of Management Learning & Education*, 22: 169–190.

Garud, R., Dunbar, R. & Bartel, C. 2011. Dealing with unusual experiences: A narrative perspective on organizational learning. *Organization Science*, 22(3): 587–601.

Geddes, D., Callister, R. & Gibson, D. 2020. A message in the madness: Functions of workplace anger in organizational life. *Academy of Management Perspectives*, 34(1): 28–47.

Gigerenzer, G. 2008. *Gut Feelings: Short Cuts to Better Decision Making*. London: Penguin.

Gill, J. & Arnold, P. 2015. Performing the principal: School leadership, masculinity and emotion. *International Journal of Leadership in Education*, 18(1): 19–33.

Gill, M. 2023. Understanding the spread of sustained employee volunteering: How volunteers influence their coworkers' moral identity work. *Journal of Management*, 49(2): 677–708.

Gilmore, S. & Kenny, K. 2015. Work-worlds colliding: Self-reflexivity, power and emotion in organizational ethnography. *Human Relations*, 68: 55–78.

Giner-Sorolla, R. 2013. *Judging Passions: Moral Emotions in Persons and Groups*. New York: Psychology Press.

Giner-Sorolla, R. 2018. A functional conflict theory of moral emotions. In: Gray, K. & Graham, J. (eds), *Atlas of Moral Psychology*, pp81–87. New York: Guilford.

Gleibs, I. & Haslam, S. 2016. Do we want a fighter? The influence of group status and the stability of intergroup relations on leader prototypicality and endorsement. *Leadership Quarterly*, 27: 557–573.

Gray, B. 2008. Putting emotion and reflexivity to work in researching migration. *Sociology*, 42: 935–952.

Greenbaum, R., Bardes Mawritz, M. & Piccolo, R. 2015. When leaders fail to "walk the talk": Supervisor undermining and perceptions of leader hypocrisy. *Journal of Management*, 41(3): 929–956.

Greenberg, D. & Hibbert, P. 2020. Learning to hope and hoping to learn. *Academy of Management Learning & Education*, 19: 123–130.

Griessmair, M. 2017. Ups and downs: Emotional dynamics in negotiations and their effects on (in)equity. *Group Decision and Negotiation*, 26: 1061–1090.

Grimes, M. 2018. The pivot: How founders respond to feedback through idea and identity work. *Academy of Management Journal*, 61(5): 1692–1717.

Hammond, M., Clapp-Smith, R. & Palanski, M. 2017. Beyond (just) the workplace: A theory of leader development across multiple domains. *Academy of Management Review*, 42(3): 481–498.

Hannah, S., Jennings, P. & Ben-Yoav Nobel, O. 2010. Tactical military leader requisite complexity: Toward a referent structure. *Military Psychology*, 22: 412–449.

Hardy, B. & Hibbert, P. 2012. Interaction, introspection and interoception: Listening to the body's voice in reflexive incidents. Presented to the Academy of Management Conference, Boston, MA.

Harris, R. 2019. *ACT Made Simple*. Oakland, CA: New Harbinger Publications.

Havermans, L., Keegan, A. & Den Hartog, D. 2015. Choosing your words carefully: Leaders' narratives of complex emergent problem resolution. *International Journal of Project Management*, 33: 973–984.

Hay, A. 2014. "I don't know what I am doing!": Surfacing struggles of managerial identity work. *Management Learning*, 45: 509–524.

Hibbert, P. 2013. Approaching reflexivity through critical reflection: Issues for critical management education. *Journal of Management Education*, 37: 803–827.

Hibbert, P. 2015. On leading in networks: The role of reflexive practices. In: Beech, N. and Gilmore, C. (eds), *Organising Music: Theory, Practice, Performance*, pp162–171. Cambridge: Cambridge University Press.

Hibbert, P. 2021a. *How to Be a Reflexive Researcher*. Cheltenham, UK and Northampton, MA, USA: Edward Elgar Publishing.

Hibbert, P. 2021b. Responsible management education research: Achievements, risks and opportunities. In: PRME (ed.) *Responsible Management Education: The PRME Global Movement*, pp370–383. London: Routledge.

Hibbert, P. 2023. Moral emotions and their functional conflicts: Effects in organizational contexts. Presented to the Academy of Management Conference, Boston, MA.

Hibbert, P., Beech, N., Callagher, L. & Siedlok, F. 2022. After the pain: Reflexive practice, emotion work and learning. *Organization Studies*, 43(5): 797–817.

Hibbert, P., Beech, N. & Siedlok, F. 2017. Leadership formation: Interpreting experience. *Academy of Management Learning & Education*, 16: 603–622.

Hibbert, P., Callagher, L., Siedlok, F., Windahl, C. & Kim, H.-S. 2019. (Engaging or avoiding) responsibility through reflexive practices. *Journal of Management Inquiry*, 28: 187–203.

Hibbert, P., Coupland C. & MacIntosh, R. 2010. Reflexivity: Recursion and relationality in organizational research processes. *Qualitative Research in Organizations and Management*, 5: 47–62.

Hibbert, P. & Cunliffe, A. 2015. Responsible management: Engaging moral reflexive practice through threshold concepts. *Journal of Business Ethics*, 127: 177–188.

Hibbert, P. & Huxham, C. 2010. The past in play: Tradition in the structures of collaboration. *Organization Studies*, 31: 525–554.

Hibbert, P. & Huxham, C. 2011. The carriage of tradition: Knowledge and its past in network contexts. *Management Learning*, 42: 7–24.

Hibbert, P., Mavin, S. & Beech, N. 2022. Enhancing the potential for leaders to learn from/in vulnerability: On the experience and practice of vulnerable reflexive dialogue. Presented to the EGOS Colloquium, Vienna.

Hibbert, P., Siedlok, F. & Beech, N. 2016. The role of interpretation in learning practices, in the context of collaboration. *Academy of Management Learning & Education*, 15: 26–44.

Hibbert, P., Sillince, J., Diefenbach, T. & Cunliffe, A. 2014. Relationally reflexive practice: A generative approach to theory development in qualitative research. *Organizational Research Methods*, 17: 278–298.

Higashida, N. 2013. *The Reason I Jump*. London: Sceptre.

Hochschild, A. 1979. Emotion work, feeling rules, and social structure. *American Journal of Sociology*, 85: 551–575.

Hoon, C., Brinkmann, J. & Baluch, A. 2023. Narrative memory work of employees in family businesses: How founding stories shape organizational identification. *Family Business Review*, 36(1): 37–62.

Hühn, M. & Meyer, M. 2023. Sophistry or wisdom in words: Aristotle on rhetoric and leadership. *Business Ethics, the Environment & Responsibility*, 32: 544–554.

Hurt, K. & Welbourne, J. 2008. Conflict and decision-making: Attributional and emotional influences. *Negotiation and Conflict Management Research*, 11(3): 225–251.

Ibarra, H. & Barbulescu, R. 2010. Identity as narrative: Prevalence, effectiveness, and consequences of narrative identity work in macro work role transitions. *Academy of Management Review*, 35: 135–154.

Immordino-Yang, M. 2016. *Emotions, Learning and the Brain*. New York: W.W. Norton & Company.

Jammaers, E. & Ybema, S. 2023. Oddity as commodity? The body as symbolic resource for other-defying identity work. *Organization Studies*, 44(5): 785–805.

Jan Verheul, W. & Schaap, L. 2010. Strong leaders? The challenges and pitfalls in mayoral leadership. *Public Administration*, 88: 439–454.

Jonason, A. 2019. Defining, aligning, and negotiating futures: New forms of identity work in an urban farming project. *Sociological Perspectives*, 62(5): 691–708.

Judson, G. 2020. Conceptualizing imagination in the context of school leadership. *International Journal of Leadership in Education*, doi: 10.1080/13603124.2020.1818289

Kane, A. & Levina, N. 2017. "Am I still one of them?": Bicultural immigrant managers navigating social identity threats when spanning global boundaries. *Journal of Management Studies*, 54(4): 540–577.

Keevers, L. & Treleaven, L. 2011. Organizing practices of reflection: A practice-based study. *Management Learning*, 42: 505–520.

Kemp, E., Cowart, K. & Bui, M. 2020. Promoting consumer well-being: Examining emotion regulation strategies in social advertising messages. *Journal of Business Research*, 112: 200–209.

Kennedy-Macfoy, M. 2013. "It's important for the students to meet someone like you": How perceptions of the researcher can affect gaining access, building rapport and securing cooperation in school-based research. *International Journal of Social Research Methodology*, 16(6): 491–502.

Kivenen, N. 2021. Writing grief, breathing hope. *Gender, Work and Organization*, 28: 497–505.

Knights, D. & Clarke, C. 2014. It's a bittersweet symphony, this life: Fragile academic selves and insecure identities at work. *Organization Studies*, 35(3): 335–357.

Korber, S., Hibbert, P., Callagher, L., Siedlok, F. & Elsahn, Z. 2023. We-experiences and the maintenance of workplace friendships: Being workplace friends together. *Management Learning*, doi: 10.1177/13505076231181194

Körner, A., Tscharaktschiew, N., Schindler, R., Schulz, K. & Rudolph, U. 2016. The everyday moral judge: Autobiographical recollections of moral emotions. *PLoS ONE*, 11(12): e0167224.

Koveshnikov, A., Vaara, E. & Ehrnrooth, M. 2016. Stereotype-based managerial identity work in multinational corporations. *Organization Studies*, 37(9): 1353–1379.

Kristjánsson, K. 2010. *The Self and Its Emotions*. Cambridge: Cambridge University Press.

Kroeze, R. & Keulen, S. 2013. Leading a multinational is history in practice: The use of invented traditions and narratives at AkzoNobel, Shell, Philips and ABN AMRO. *Business History*, 55: 1265–1287.

Küpers, W. & Pauleen, D. 2015. Learning wisdom: Embodied and artful approaches to management education. *Scandinavian Journal of Management*, 31: 493–500.

Kyratsis, Y., Atun, R., Phillips, N., Tracey, P. & George, G. 2017. Health systems in transition: Professional identity work in the context of shifting institutional logics. *Academy of Management Journal*, 60(2): 610–641.

Ladge, J., Clair, J. & Greenberg, D. 2012. Cross-domain identity transition during liminal periods: Constructing multiple selves as professional and mother during pregnancy. *Academy of Management Journal*, 55(6): 1449–1471.

Ladge, J. & Little, L. 2019. When expectations become reality: Work–family image management and identity adaptation. *Academy of Management Review*, 44(1): 126–149.

Laing, C. & Moules, N. 2014. Stories from cancer camp: Tales of glitter and gratitude. *Journal of Applied Hermeneutics*, 3.

Larsson, M. & Knudsen, M. 2022. Conditions for reflexive practices in leadership learning: The regulating role of a socio-moral order of peer interactions. *Management Learning*, 53(2): 291–309.

Le Guin, U. 1969. *The Left Hand of Darkness*. New York: Ace Books.

Leder, D. 2019. Inside insights: A phenomenology of interoception. In: Tsakiris, M. & De Preester, H. (eds), *The Interoceptive Mind*, pp307–322. Oxford: Oxford University Press.

Lee, Y.-H. & Lin, H. 2011. "Gaming is my work": Identity work in internet-hobbyist game workers. *Work, Employment and Society*, 25(3): 451–467.

Lees-Marshment, J. & Smolović Jones, O. 2018. Being more with less: Exploring the flexible political leadership identities of government ministers. *Leadership*, 14(4): 460–482.

Leigh, J. & Brown, N. 2021. *Embodied Inquiry*. London: Bloomsbury.

Leverage, P., Mancing, H., Schweickert, R. & Marston Williams, J. 2011. *Theory of Mind and Literature*. West Lafayette, IN: Purdue University Press.

Ligon, G.S., Hunter, S.T. & Mumford, M.D. 2008. Development of outstanding leadership: A life narrative approach. *Leadership Quarterly*, 19: 312–334.

Lindebaum, D. 2017. *Emancipation through Emotion Regulation at Work*. Cheltenham, UK and Northampton, MA, USA: Edward Elgar Publishing.

Lindebaum, D. & Gabriel, Y. 2016. Anger and organization studies: From social disorder to moral order. *Organization Studies*, 37(7): 903–918.

Long, Z., Linabary, J., Buzzanell, P., Mouton, A. & Rao, R. 2020. Enacting everyday feminist collaborations: Reflexive becoming, proactive improvisation and co-learning partnerships. *Gender, Work and Organization*, 27: 487–506.

Lupu, I., Spence, C. & Empson, L. 2018. When the past comes back to haunt you: The enduring influence of upbringing on the work–family decisions of professional parents. *Human Relations*, 71: 155–181.

Maclean, M., Harvey, C. & Chia, R. 2012. Reflexive practice and the making of elite business careers. *Management Learning*, 43: 385–404.

Maclean, M., Harvey, C., Golant, B. & Sillince, J. 2021. The role of innovation narratives in accomplishing organizational ambidexterity. *Strategic Organization*, 19(4): 693–721.

Maitlis, S. 2020. Posttraumatic growth at work. *Annual Review of Organizational Psychology and Organizational Behavior*, 7: 395–419.

Mar, R. 2018. Stories and the promotion of social cognition. *Current Directions in Psychological Science*, 27(4): 257–262.

Mar, R., Li, J., Nguyen, A. & Ta, C. 2021. Memory and comprehension of narrative versus expository texts: A meta-analysis. *Psychonomic Bulletin & Review*, 28: 732–749.

McGivern, G., Currie, G., Ferlie, E., Fitzgerald, L. & Waring, J. 2015. Hybrid manager–professionals' identity work: The maintenance and hybridization of medical professionalism in managerial contexts. *Public Administration*, 93(2): 412–432.

Meister, A., Jehn, K. & Thatcher, S. 2014. Feeling misidentified: The consequences of internal identity asymmetries for individuals at work. *Academy of Management Review*, 39(4): 488–512.

Meister, A., Sinclair, A. & Jehn, K. 2017. Identities under scrutiny: How women leaders navigate feeling misidentified at work. *Leadership Quarterly*, 28(5): 672–690.

Mills, C.W. 1959. *The Sociological Imagination*. Oxford: Oxford University Press.

Mills, T. & Kleinman, S. 1988. Emotions, reflexivity and action: An interactionist analysis. *Social Forces*, 66: 1009–1027.

Mirvis, P. & Ayas, K. 2003. Reflective dialogue, life stories, and leadership development. *Reflections*, 4(4): 39–48.

Miscenko, D., Guenter, H. & Day, D. 2017. Am I a leader? Examining leader identity development over time. *Leadership Quarterly*, 28(5): 605–620.

Mittal, R. & Dorfman, P. 2012. Servant leadership across cultures. *Journal of World Business*, 47(4): 555–570.

Muhr, S.L., De Cock, C., Twardowska, M. & Volkmann, C. 2019. Constructing an entrepreneurial life: Liminality and emotional reflexivity in identity work. *Entrepreneurship & Regional Development*, 31(7/8): 567–582.

Myers, K. 2010. *Reflexive Practice: Professional Thinking for a Turbulent World*. New York: Palgrave Macmillan.

Namatende-Sakwa, L. 2018. "Madam, are you one of them?": "Reflexivities of discomfort" in researching an "illicit" subject. *International Journal of Qualitative Studies in Education*, 31: 328–340.

Nichols, R. 2009. Research and Indigenous participation: Critical reflexive methods. *International Journal of Social Research Methodology*, 12: 117–126.

Niven, K., Totterdell, P., Holman, D. & Headley, T. 2012. Does regulating others' feelings influence people's own affective well-being? *Journal of Social Psychology*, 152: 246–260.

O'Reilly, C., Chatman, J. & Doerr, B. 2021. When "me" trumps "we": Narcissistic leaders and the cultures they create. *Academy of Management Discoveries*, 7(3): 419–450.

Orr, K. & Bennett, M. 2016. Relational leadership, storytelling, and narratives: Practices of local government chief executives. *Public Administration Review*, 77(4): 515–527.

Palmer, P. 2009. *A Hidden Wholeness*. San Francisco, CA: Jossey Bass.

Palmer, W. & Crawford, J. 2013. *Leadership Embodiment*. San Rafael, CA: CreateSpace.

Parker, S. 2022. *Embracing Unrest*. Vancouver: PageTwo.

Parkinson, B. & Manstead, A. 2015. Current emotion research in social psychology: Thinking about emotions and other people. *Emotion Review*, 7(4): 371–380.

Parry, K. & Kempster, S. 2014. Love and leadership: Constructing follower narrative identities of charismatic leadership. *Management Learning*, 45: 21–38.

Paton, S., Chia, R. & Burt, G. 2014. Relevance or "relevate"? How university business schools can add value through reflexively learning from strategic partnerships with business. *Management Learning*, 45(3): 267–288.

Perrott, T. 2019. Doing hot and "dirty" work: Masculinities and occupational identity in firefighting. *Gender Work and Organization*, 26: 1398–1412.

Perry, M. & Medina, C.L. (eds) 2015. *Methodologies of Embodiment: Inscribing Bodies in Qualitative Research*. London: Routledge.

Petrieglieri, G., Ashford, S. & Wrzesniewski, A. 2019. Agony and ecstasy in the gig economy: Cultivating holding environments for precarious and personalized work identities. *Administrative Science Quarterly*, 64(1): 124–170.

Petriglieri, G. & Petriglieri, J. 2010. Identity workspaces: The case of business schools. *Academy of Management Learning & Education*, 9: 44–60.

Petriglieri, G. & Petriglieri, J. 2015. Can business schools humanize leadership? *Academy of Management Learning & Education*, 14: 625–647.

Pless, N., Sengupta, A., Wheeler, M. & Maak, T. 2022. Responsible leadership and the reflective CEO: Resolving stakeholder conflict by imagining what could be done. *Journal of Business Ethics*, 180: 313–337.

Polanyi, M. 1966. *The Tacit Dimension*. New York: Doubleday.

Quadt, L., Critchley, H. & Garfinkel, S. 2019. Interoception and emotion: Shared mechanisms and clinical implications. In: Tsakiris, M. & De Preester, H. (eds), *The Interoceptive Mind*, pp123–143. Oxford: Oxford University Press.

Quintard, V., Jouffe, S., Hommel, B. & Bouquet, C. 2021. Embodied self–other overlap in romantic love: A review and integrative perspective. *Psychological Research*, 85: 899–914.

Raelin, J. 2007. Toward an epistemology of practice. *Academy of Management Learning & Education*, 6: 495–519.

Raelin, J. (ed.). 2016. *Leadership as Practice*. London: Routledge.

Rain, M. & Mar, R. 2021. Adult attachment and engagement with fictional characters. *Journal of Social and Personal Relationships*, 38(9): 2792–2813.

Ramsey, C. 2008. Managing to learn: The social poetics of a polyphonic classroom. *Organization Studies*, 24(4): 543–558.

Ramsey, R. 2011. On the dire necessity of the useless: Philosophical and rhetorical thoughts on hermeneutics and education in the humanities. In P. Fairfield (ed.), *Education, Dialogue and Hermeneutics*, pp91–106. London: Continuum.

Rehman Khan, S. 2021. Different and better than you: The interplay between social identity, moral identity, and social comparison. *Journal of Community & Applied Social Psychology*, 31: 615–635.

Reichard, R.J. & Johnson, S.K. 2011. Leader self-development as organizational strategy. *Leadership Quarterly*, 22, 33–42.

Rhodes, C. & Carlsen, A. 2018. The teaching of the other: Ethical vulnerability and generous reciprocity in the research process. *Human Relations*, 71: 1295–1318.

Riach, K. & Cutcher, L. 2014. Built to last: Ageing, class and the masculine body in a UK hedge fund. *Work, Employment and Society*, 28(5): 771–787.

Rigg, C. 2018. Somatic learning: Bringing the body into critical reflection. *Management Learning,* 49: 150–167.

Ripamonti, S., Galuppo, L., Gorli, M., Scaratti, G. & Cunliffe, A.L. 2017. Pushing action research toward reflexive practice. *Journal of Management Inquiry,* 25: 55–68.

Rothman, J. 2014. Reflexive pedagogy: Teaching and learning in peace and conflict studies. *Conflict Resolution Quarterly,* 32(2): 109–120.

Saam, N. 2018. Recognizing the emotion work in deliberation: Why emotions do not make deliberative democracy more democratic. *Political Psychology,* 39(4): 755–774.

Saggurthi, S. & Thakur, M. 2016. Usefulness of uselessness: A case for negative capability in management. *Academy of Management Learning & Education,* 15(1): 180–193.

Schachter, S. & Singer, J. 1962. Cognitive, social, and physiological determinants of emotional state. *Psychological Review,* 69: 379–399.

Schedlitzki, D., Edwards, G. & Kempster, S. 2018. The absent follower: Identity construction within organisationally assigned leader–follower relations. *Leadership,* 14(4): 483–503.

Schedlitzki, D., Jarvis, C. & MacInnes, J. 2015. Leadership development: A place for storytelling and Greek mythology? *Management Learning,* 46: 412–426.

Schnall, S., Haidt, J., Clore, G.L., & Jordan, A.H. 2008. Disgust as embodied moral judgment. *Personality and Social Psychology Bulletin,* 34(8): 1096–1109.

Scott, B.A., Awasty, N., Johnson, R.E., Matta, F.K. & Hollenbeck, J.R. 2020. Origins and destinations, distances and directions: Accounting for the journey in the emotion regulation process. *Academy of Management Review,* 45(2): 423–446.

Sela-Sheffy, R. & Leshem, R. 2016. Emotion-identity talk in aggressive interactions and in reflexive accounts. *Culture & Psychology,* 22: 448–466.

Shams, F. 2019. Managing academic identity tensions in a Canadian public university: The role of identity work in coping with managerialism. *Journal of Higher Education Policy and Management,* 41(6): 619–632.

Sharvit, K., Brambilla, M., Babush, M. & Colucci, F.P. 2015. To feel or not to feel when my group harms others? The regulation of collective guilt as motivated reasoning. *Personality and Social Psychology Bulletin,* 41(9): 1223–1235.

Shepherd, D. & Williams, T. 2016. Hitting rock bottom after job loss: Bouncing back to create a new positive work identity. *Academy of Management Review*, 43(1): 28–49.

Shils, E. 1981. *Tradition*. Chicago, IL: University of Chicago Press.

Shoup, J. & Hinrichs, T. 2021. *Literature and Leadership*. Abingdon: Routledge.

Simon, G. 2013. Relational ethnography: Writing and reading in research relationships. *Forum: Qualitative Social Research*, 14: Article 4.

Sirén, C., He, V., Wesemann, H., Jonassen, Z., Grichnik, D. & von Krogh, G. 2020. Leader emergence in nascent venture teams: The critical roles of individual emotion regulation and team emotions. *Journal of Management Studies*, 57(5): 931–961.

Sklaveniti, C. & Steyaert, C. 2020. Reflecting with Pierre Bourdieu: Towards a reflexive outlook for practice-based studies of entrepreneurship. *Entrepreneurship & Regional Development*, 32: 313–333.

Smith, N. & Fredricks-Lowman, I. 2020. Conflict in the workplace: A 10-year review of toxic leadership in higher education. *International Journal of Leadership in Education*, 23(5): 538–551.

Soini, A. & Eräranta, K. 2023. Collaborative construction of the closet (in and out): The affordance of interactivity and gay and lesbian employees' identity work online. *Organization*, 30(1): 21–41.

Sparrowe, R. 2005. Authentic leadership and the narrative self. *Leadership Quarterly*, 16: 419–439.

Stark, J., Reif, J. & Schiebler, T. 2022. What leaders tell and employees hear: An intention-perception model of storytelling in leadership. *Organization Management Journal*, 19(2): 72–83.

Stead, V. & Elliott, C. 2012. Women's leadership learning: A reflexive review of representations and leadership teaching. *Management Learning*, 44(4): 373–394.

Steele, L. & Lovelace, J. 2023. Organizational underdog narratives: The cultivation and consequences of a collective underdog identity. *Academy of Management Review*, 48(1): 32–56.

Steffens, P., Baker, T., Davidsson, P. & Senyard, J. 2023. When is less more? Boundary conditions of effective entrepreneurial bricolage. *Journal of Management*, 49(4): 1277–1311.

Steinbock, A. 2014. *Moral Emotions: Reclaiming the Evidence of the Heart*. Evanston, IL: Northwestern University Press.

Stenholm, P. & Renko, M. 2016. Passionate bricoleurs and new venture survival. *Journal of Business Venturing*, 31: 595–611.

Sternberg, R. 2008. The WICS approach to leadership: Stories of leadership and the structures and processes that support them. *Leadership Quarterly*, 19(3): 360–371.

Sunduramurthy, C., Zheng, C., Musteen, M., Francis, J. & Rhyne, L. 2016. Doing more with less, systematically? Bricolage and ingenieuring in successful social ventures. *Journal of World Business*, 51: 855–870.

Sutherland, I. 2013. Arts-based methods in leadership development: Affording aesthetic workspaces, reflexivity and memories with momentum. *Management Learning*, 44: 25–43.

Sveningsson, S. & Alvesson, M. 2003. Managing managerial identities: Organizational fragmentation, discourse and identity struggle. *Human Relations*, 56(10): 1163–1193.

Sveningsson, S. & Larsson, M. 2006. Fantasies of leadership: Identity work. *Leadership*, 2(2): 203–224.

Sydow, J., Lerch, F., Huxham, C. & Hibbert, P. 2011. A silent cry for leadership: Organizing for leading (in) clusters. *Leadership Quarterly*, 22: 328–343.

Tangney, J.P., Stuewig, J. & Mashek, D.J. 2007. Moral emotions and moral behavior. *Annual Review of Psychology*, 58(1): 345–372.

Taylor, S.S. & Ladkin, D. 2009. Understanding arts-based methods in managerial development. *Academy of Management Learning and Education*, 8: 55–69.

Tedeschi, R.G., Shakespeare-Finch, J., Taku, K. & Calhoun, L.G. 2018. *Posttraumatic Growth: Theory, Research, and Applications*. New York: Routledge.

Tee, E. 2015. The emotional link: Leadership and the role of implicit and explicit emotional contagion processes across multiple organizational levels. *Leadership Quarterly*, 26: 654–670.

Thompson, N. 2018. Imagination and creativity in organizations. *Organization Studies*, 39(2–3): 229–250.

Tienari, J. 2022. Academic work and imagination: Reflections of an armchair traveler. *Management Learning*, doi: 10.1177/13505076221136932

Treviño, L. & Brown, M. 2004. Managing to be ethical: Debunking five business ethics myths. *Academy of Management Perspectives*, 18: 69–81.

Troth, A., Lawrence, S., Jordan, P. & Ashkanasy, N. 2018. Interpersonal emotion regulation in the workplace: A conceptual and operational review and future research agenda. *International Journal of Management Reviews*, 20: 523–543.

Troth, A., Townsend, K., Loudoun, R. & Burgess, M. 2023. Frontline managers' task-related emotion regulation, emotional intelligence, and daily stress. *Australian Journal of Management*, 48(1): 108–129.

Tsakiris, M. & De Preester, H. (eds). 2019. *The Interoceptive Mind*. Oxford: Oxford University Press.

Ullrich, J., Christ, O. & Van Dick, R. 2009. Substitutes for procedural fairness: Prototypical leaders are endorsed whether they are fair or not. *Journal of Applied Psychology*, 94(1): 235–244.

Vaara, T. & Tienari, J. 2011. On the narrative construction of multinational corporations: An antenarrative analysis of legitimation and resistance in a cross-border merger. *Organization Science*, 22: 370–390.

Van den Bergh, O., Zacharioudakis, N. & Petersen, S. 2019. Interoception, categorization and symptom perception. In: Tsakiris, M. & De Preester, H. (eds), *The Interoceptive Mind*, pp212–226. Oxford: Oxford University Press.

Van der Kolk, B. 2015. *The Body Keeps the Score*. London: Penguin Random House.

Van Kleef, G.A. 2014. Understanding the positive and negative effects of emotional expressions in organizations: EASI does it. *Human Relations*, 67, 1145–1164.

Van Knippenberg, D., Van Knippenberg, B., De Cremer, D. & Hogg, M.A. 2004. Leadership, self, and identity: A review and research agenda. *Leadership Quarterly*, 15(6): 825–856.

Walsh, M. 2021. *The Body in Coaching and Training: An Introduction to Embodied Facilitation*. London: Open University Press.

Warren, M., Sekhon, T., Winkelman, K. & Waldrop, R. 2022. Should I "check my emotions at the door" or express how I feel? Role of emotion regulation versus expression of male leaders speaking out against sexism in the workplace. *Journal of Applied Social Psychology*, 52(7): 547–558.

Weinsheimer, J. 2004. Meaningless hermeneutics? In: Krajewski, B. (ed.), *Gadamer's Repercussions*, pp158–166. Berkeley, CA: University of California Press.

Wesley, J. 2002. Growing up sexualized: Issues of power and violence in the lives of female exotic dancers. *Violence against Women*, 8(10): 1182–1207.

Wijaya, H. & Heugens, P. 2018. Give me a hallelujah! Amen! Institutional reproduction in the presence of moral perturbation and the dynamics of emotional investment. *Organization Studies*, 39(4): 491–514.

Williams, M. & Penman, D. 2011. *Mindfulness*. London: Piatkus.

Wilson, T. 2004. *Strangers to Ourselves: Discovering the Adaptive Unconscious*. Cambridge, MA: Belknap Press of Harvard University Press.

Winkler, I. 2018. Identity work and emotions: A review. *International Journal of Management Reviews*, 20(1): 120–133.

Wittman, M. & Meissner, K. 2019. The embodiment of time: How interoception shapes the perception of time. In: Tsakiris, M. & De Preester, H. (eds), *The Interoceptive Mind*, pp63–79. Oxford: Oxford University Press.

Wolfram Cox, J. & Hassard, J. 2018. From relational to relationist leadership in critical management education: Recasting leadership work after the practice turn. *Academy of Management Learning & Education*, 17: 532–556.

Wright, A., Middleton, S., Hibbert, P. & Brazil, V. 2020. Getting on with field research using participant deconstruction. *Organizational Research Methods*, 23(2): 275–295.

Yakhlef, A. 2010. The corporeality of practice-based learning. *Organization Studies*, 31(4): 409–430.

Yang, I. & Yeh, C. 2023. A place and time for humor: Leader humor in Confucian cultures. *Journal of Management & Organization*, 29: 122–138.

Yip, J., Trainor, L., Black, H., Soto-Torres, L. & Reichard, R. 2020. Coaching new leaders: A relational process of integrating multiple identities. *Academy of Management Learning & Education*, 19: 503–520.

Zaar, S. Van Den Bossche, P. & Gijselaers, W. 2020. How business students think about leadership: A qualitative study on leader identity and meaning-making. *Academy of Management Learning & Education*, 19: 168–191.

Zak, P. & Winn, B. 2016. *Your Body at Work: Physiology, Neuroscience, and Leadership. People & Strategy*, 39(2): 58–61.

Zembylas, M. 2007. Mobilizing anger for social justice: The politicization of the emotions in education. *Teaching Education*, 18(1): 15–28.

INDEX

Note: **Bold** page numbers refer to tables, *italic* page numbers refer to figures and page numbers followed by "n" refer to end notes.

moral role models 115, 126
motivations 101; non-conscious 13,
    103
movement, mindful 30, 33
multiple identities 135
muscular leadership 118

narratives: coherence 101–104;
    conceptualization 131; genres
    136–137; official 137; organizational
    15, 131–133; organizational learning
    role 132; power of 131–139;
    public forms 136–139; roles 132;
    self 15, 101–104, 105, 116, 128,
    133–136, 140–141; storylines 73;
    underground 137
natural sciences 20
negative capability 12, 78–80, 84
nervous system 23, 24, 25–26
neurodivergent people 26
Nikolova, N. 18, 19
non-conscious behaviors 87
non-conscious motivations 13
non-directive influence 3
non-utilitarian education 7
non-work interests 7
norms: changing 125–126;
    disadvantaging 51; tacit 48
not knowing 79–80; normality of 6

online meeting technologies 96
open mind 143
opinions, sharing 94
opportunity 2
option overload 75
organizational change 15
organizational climate and culture 12,
    59–60, 62, 111–112, 132, 137
organizational learning, role of
    narratives 132
organizational life, emotions and
    56–57

organizational narratives 15, 131–133
organizational setting, and
    embodiment 21–22
organizational stories 6
organizational values 103
Orr, K. 131, 138–139
others and otherness, engaging 9, 90
outward work 3, 4, 145

pain 26, 28
Palmer, W. 35–37
Parker, S. 55
passive transmission, resisting 67
past experience: examining 71–74;
    link to 65–68
pathos 146
Paton, S. 141–142
Penman, D. 30–31, 37
performance feedback 58
personal problems 11
physical skills 74
Pitsis, A. 18, 19
planning 2
polarization 53
political leaders 118–119
postponed emotion work 43
post-traumatic stress 43
potential leaders 117
power 3
precarious identities 108–109
privilege 67
professional detachment 42
professional training 7
professional values 112
proprioception 20, 21–22, 29
prototypical person, the 127
psychological trauma 43
public management 132

Quadt, L. 27
questions, inward-focused 10
Quintard, V. 21

rational argument, appeal based on 146

rational detachment 41

reading 99, 104, 139; engagement with 96–97

real problems, encounters with 8

reflexive dialogue 9, 15, 130, 139–144; breadth 144; critical engagement 141; curiosity-driven 143–144; flexibility 144; humility 143; instrumental exchange 143; involving others 142–143; modes of engagement 143–144; open mind 143

reflexive heuristics 145, 147–148

reflexive learning 49, 142

reflexive practice 5, 6, 9–10, 21, 120, 142, 147; cultivating 29; identity and identity work 127; integrating 121–123, **123**; inward work 14; levels 9; not therapy 43; ongoing commitment 145; and organizational change 15; relevance 145; understanding 10; see also embodied reflexive practice; emotional reflexive practice; relational reflexive practice; thoughtful reflexive practice

reflexive practice groups 61–62

reflexive reception 90–92

regrets 63

rehumanization 100

Reif, J. 138

relational reflexive practice 9, 13, 14, 92, 92–99, 123, **123**, 139–140, 148; autobiographical note sharing 93, 97–99; dialogue 92, 93–96, 99, 105; and leader work 99–104; textual conversation partners 92–93, 96–97

relational reflexivity 92, 104–105; and vulnerability 100–101

relationships 85–92, 104–105; benefits 85; changed 71; critical insights through 9; and dialogue 90–92; insights through 87–92; motivational effects 89–90; trusting 94; web of 88; see also relational reflexive practice

relaxation 31, 34

relaxation techniques 33

Renko, M. 79–80

reputation 2

responsibility, and leadership 1–2, 4

rewards 146–147

Ripamonti, S. 78

role models 115, 117, 126

romantic relationships 21

Schedlitzki, D. 132

Schiebler, T. 138

Scott, B.A. 54

secondary anger 53

seeing, ways of 9

self: changed 71, 134–135; sense of 19, 108, 110, 133

self-awareness 21, 29; insights through relationships 87–92

self care 37

self-deception 50

self-development 7, 129–130, 149

self-examination 3, 65

self-expression 14, 15, 119

self-knowledge 5, 85–86

self-narratives 15, 105, 116, 128, 133–136, 140–141; coherence 101–104

self-overlap 21

self-presentation 5, 14, 108–109, 110

self-reflexivity 49, 59, 65; future orientated 68–71

self-regulation 46–47

Printed in the United Kingdom
by Rawat & Stale, Publisher Services

Printed in the United States
by Baker & Taylor Publisher Services